BREAKING SUICIDAL THOUGHTS

Exposing the Spiritual War on the Mind and the Path to Lasting Freedom

Dennis E. Ofori

This book is a spiritual and theological resource. It is meant for educational and devotional purposes. While every effort has been made to ensure biblical accuracy, readers are encouraged to test all teachings against Scripture and seek the leading of the Holy Spirit

Table of Contents

DEDICATION

To the Holy Trinity and all the Angels of God that have ever walked with me or Intervened in my life. I say Thank you!

I am forever grateful!

Author's Note

I did not write this book because I am strong. I wrote it because I have been weak, broken, tired, and weary of life. There were seasons when everything in me wanted to give up. I tried to live right. I prayed. I fasted. I fought to remain holy. Yet the more I tried, the heavier life felt. Nothing seemed to make sense. Pain filled my heart. Sorrow weighed on my soul. And many times, I thought about ending it all.

But as close as I came to that edge, I never crossed it. Not because I was better than anyone else, but because I knew what was waiting on the other side. I have seen too much of the *spirit world* to believe that suicide ends pain. I know what lurks behind that decision, what waits for the soul that leaves before its time. And that knowledge alone kept me alive.

That is why I wrote *Breaking Suicidal Thoughts*. Because I don't want you to step into what cannot be undone. I don't want you to make a choice that will echo in eternity. I want you to see what I saw, to know what I know, that there is still hope, even in the deepest night.

If you have found this book, it is not an accident. Heaven wanted you to. You may not feel it, but you are being pursued by mercy. I have written this book through tears, through battles, through spiritual warfare that nearly broke me. I have seen the darkness that whispers death, and the Light that whispers life.

God has taken me through things few ever talk about, showing me truths that most never write down. But I did. I wrote them all, the revelations, the visions, the lessons, so that someone like you would find them when you needed them most.

You see, I didn't take my life. I stayed. I fought. And today, you are reading my book. Tomorrow, I want to read yours. I want to hear your testimony. I want to see how you turned your pain into purpose, how you built something beautiful out of your ashes.

You are not a mistake. You are a mission. You are not forgotten, you are being written into a story that still matters.

So before you say goodbye… please, *stay.* There is more waiting for you than you can imagine.

. Dennis E. Ofori

Introduction

Suicide is not merely a mental health crisis. It is a spiritual crisis. It is a collision between pain and deception, between despair and a demonic voice that whispers, "End it all." Every day, countless souls walk to the edge of eternity, haunted by demons that the human eye cannot see and burdened by pain too deep for language. The world tries to explain suicide through clinical terminology, chemical imbalances, trauma histories, social disconnection, but behind the curtain of the physical lies a greater and often ignored truth: suicide is influenced and, in many cases, driven by spiritual forces of darkness.

This book is not written for casual reading. It is a wake-up call. It is a trumpet blast in the spirit realm. If you are holding this book in your hands, then God is trying to speak to you, whether you're the one struggling with thoughts of suicide, someone who has lost a loved one, or a spiritual leader looking to understand the deeper realities of this tragic epidemic. You are not here by accident. There is a divine interruption taking place in your life, right now, as your eyes move across these words.

Many who take their own lives don't do so because they want to die. They simply want the pain to stop. They are exhausted from carrying wounds they've never been able to heal, thoughts they've never been able to silence, and fears they've never been able to overcome. But what most don't realize is that their thoughts are not always their own. A subtle invasion occurs in the soul, a whisper here, a suggestion there, and before long, the spirit of suicide wraps itself around a person like a fog. It clouds judgment, deadens hope, and offers the ultimate deception: "Peace comes after death."

But that is not what the Bible teaches. Peace is found only in the presence of Jesus Christ, not in escape, not in self-harm, not in death. Jesus came to bring life and life more abundantly (John 10:10). The enemy comes to kill, steal, and destroy, and suicide is one of his most successful strategies.

Our world today is filled with knowledge but starving for truth. Mental health initiatives have increased, therapy is more accessible, awareness is higher than ever, but so are suicide rates. Why? Because we have addressed the symptoms while ignoring the spiritual root. You can counsel a soul, but you cannot counsel a demon. Some forms of suicidal ideation are driven by demonic oppression, tormenting spirits, generational curses, and soul wounds that require deliverance, not just dialogue. Until we confront the reality of spiritual warfare, we will continue to bury sons, daughters, pastors, and prophets who could have been delivered if someone had only seen the invisible battle raging around them.

This book is not merely theological; it is prophetic. It's not just for education, it's for transformation. It is for the person silently fighting in their mind at 2:00 AM, feeling worthless, alone, and unseen. It is for the believer who loves Jesus but can't understand why the weight of despair never lifts. It is for those left behind, mourning a suicide and wondering what happened in the final moments. It is for pastors who have never been taught how to discern the difference between mental illness and spiritual bondage.

Every chapter you read is soaked in prayer. Every word is written under the weight of spiritual burden. We are at war, beloved. And war requires strategy. War requires clarity. War requires light shining in darkness.

For too long, the Church has either remained silent about suicide or responded with shallow clichés. "Just have more faith." "God works all things for good." "They're in a better place now." These phrases, though sometimes well-meaning, do not deal with the demonic oppression, soul fragmentation, or spiritual confusion that often underlie suicidal behavior. The Church must rise with power, compassion, and discernment. We must not only pray, we must understand. We must not only sympathize, we must intervene.

God is calling His people back to the authority of the Spirit. We must be able to identify when a soul is under siege. When someone is being harassed by a spirit of death, it is not enough to prescribe medication or positive affirmations. Those may bring temporary relief, but unless the spirit is cast out and the soul restored by God's truth, the darkness returns, often stronger than before.

Most people live unaware of the spirit realm that exists just beyond the veil of the natural. Yet the Bible makes it clear: what is unseen is eternal (2 Corinthians 4:18). There are angels. There are demons. There is warfare. And there are doors, spiritual openings through which light or darkness can enter. Suicide is often the result of an open door, whether from trauma, abuse, unforgiveness, occult activity, or prolonged emotional suffering. Demons are legalists. They look for access points. And once granted access, they operate with cunning precision. The voice of suicide is not random. It is rehearsed. It has spoken the same lies to millions of people across generations.

But this book will expose every lie. We will walk through what happens in the mind, in the soul, and in the spirit. We will uncover how suicide starts as a seed, grows into a thought pattern, becomes a torment, and ends in death, unless interrupted. That interruption can be you, right now, reading these words. That interruption can be the light of God's truth entering your mind like a holy fire.

If you're reading this and battling suicidal thoughts, you are not crazy. You are not alone. And you are not beyond help. But you must understand, there is more going on than meets the eye. You are not just struggling with thoughts. You are under attack. And just as real as the darkness feels, there is One greater who is already fighting for you.

Jesus did not come to condemn you. He came to deliver you. He did not come to lecture you. He came to rescue you. The Spirit of God is moving even now, as you read. Deliverance is not some outdated ritual. It is the violent mercy of God breaking chains and silencing spirits that have had access to your life for far too long. Some of you will find freedom in the pages ahead. Others may need to reach out for prayer and deliverance. That's not a sign of weakness, it's a sign of wisdom. Even Jesus, in His darkest hour, cried out to the Father. You can too.

We urge you: do not walk through this book alone. Pray. Ask the Holy Spirit to open your understanding. If you begin to feel agitation, heaviness, or resistance while reading, know that it is the enemy reacting to exposure. Keep going. Light is breaking in.

To the Church: rise up in discernment. Stop explaining away every torment with psychology. Use wisdom, yes, but also walk in power. Learn to discern the difference between a wounded soul and a bound one. Learn to war in the Spirit. God is raising up deliverers in this hour, and you may be one of them.

To the broken: you are not worthless. You are not too far gone. The enemy wants to destroy you because of the glory you carry. He wants to silence you before your voice breaks chains for others. Don't give him that satisfaction. Live. Fight. Cry if you must. But stay. There is redemption coming for you.

To the called: some of you reading this know deep down that you are meant to help others. You've seen too much pain. You've lost friends or family to suicide. Maybe you've even attempted it yourself. But God is turning your scars into swords. Your story will set captives free. This book is not just for your healing, it's for your commissioning.

We are living in an age where truth is increasingly rejected in favor of comfort, where sin is explained away and darkness is tolerated rather than confronted. Suicide is one of the subjects where this compromise has had deadly consequences. Instead of calling out the demonic spirit that drives it, we label it purely as a "mental health condition" and move on. But make no mistake. Satan loves silence. He thrives in the places where the Church is afraid to speak plainly.

Yes, we grieve with those who have lost loved ones to suicide. Yes, we honor their pain and their humanity. But we must also declare: the truth sets free (John 8:32). And the truth is that suicide is not a natural solution, it is a supernatural deception. When the Church fails to confront the real source, it leaves the people defenseless. When we reduce spiritual battles to psychological conditions, we put band-aids on bullet wounds.

It's time to restore the ministry of deliverance to its rightful place. It's time to recognize that what cannot be counseled must be cast out. This is not cruelty, it is compassion. What sense does it make to spend years in therapy while ignoring the tormentor whispering in your ear every night? Some of you reading this have tried everything, medication, therapy, new environments, self-help, but the voices haven't stopped. That's because the root is spiritual. And it requires spiritual intervention.

Let us be clear: suicide does not usher anyone into peace. It is not a gateway to heaven unless that person had truly surrendered their life to Jesus Christ. And even then, suicide is never God's will. It is the final act of rebellion against the gift of life. It's not romantic. It's not noble. It's not a "release." It is a premature entry into the spirit realm, often guided by the very demon who deceived the soul into it.

This is why the enemy fights so hard to normalize suicidal thoughts. He glamorizes death. He disguises despair as "freedom." He lies and says, "No one will miss you," "You're a burden," "You've gone too far," "This is the only way out." And when someone believes that lie long enough, the demon behind it moves in for the kill.

In Scripture, the spirit of death and destruction was always active wherever God's people refused to walk in truth. In Mark 9, a young boy is tormented by an unclean spirit that causes seizures and tries to throw him into fire and water to destroy him. What does Jesus do? He casts it out. That's our model. That's the standard. That's the missing piece in most modern discussions on suicide, we are trying to psychoanalyze what must be spiritually confronted.

God is raising up watchmen in this hour. You are not reading this by accident. If you are a parent, pastor, friend, counselor, or even just a believer with spiritual sensitivity, it's time to watch and pray like never before. The spirit of suicide is creeping through our homes, our schools, our churches, and yes, even our pulpits.

It targets the isolated, the rejected, the gifted, and the called. It doesn't care about age, gender, race, or social status. It only cares about extinguishing destiny. If you feel led to intercede for someone, don't wait. If you discern a heaviness around someone, speak up. If someone you love suddenly changes, withdraws, gives away possessions, makes morbid jokes, don't dismiss it. Fast. Pray. Confront the darkness. Love them with truth and boldness.

The spirit realm is real. And while we don't live in fear, we must live in awareness. We are soldiers in a spiritual war, not tourists in a broken world.

Maybe you're reading this right now and you're the one on the edge. Maybe no one knows what you're battling. Maybe you've smiled through the pain, prayed but felt nothing, and you're starting to believe the lie that says, "God doesn't care." Let us be clear: God cares deeply. And He brought you to this moment to interrupt your descent.

You are not reading these words by chance. You could have picked any book, watched any video, talked to any person, but instead, you're here. That means the Spirit of God is reaching out to you. He is not angry with you. He is not disappointed. He is standing at the door of your heart, not with a fist, but with a scarred hand that was pierced for your pain.

Jesus understands anguish. He understands betrayal, abandonment, isolation, and even despair. In the Garden of Gethsemane, He cried out in agony. On the cross, He said, "My God, why have You forsaken Me?" He has been where you are. But He didn't quit. He didn't give in. He finished the mission, so that you could have the strength to finish yours.

This book will teach you about the spirit realm, the human soul, the afterlife, and the lies that destroy lives. But more than that, it will walk you toward freedom. Deliverance is possible. That demonic spirit that has tormented you for years can be driven out by the name and blood of Jesus. You don't have to live with the weight forever.

You may need more than just this book. You may need personal ministry. That's okay. We've included resources at the end. Reach out. Pray. Fast. Ask the Holy Spirit to guide you to the right people. We are not just writing to you, we are fighting for you.

If the Lord wills, we will pray with you. We will stand with you. We will contend until you are free. This is not just information, it's an invitation to breakthrough.

Pastor, leader, minister, this is your time to reclaim the fire. Don't just preach what is safe. Preach what sets captives free. Don't just hold services, break chains. Bring back the altars. Cast out devils. Raise up deliverance teams. Don't outsource everything to therapists and counselors, raise up Spirit-filled intercessors and warriors. Many churches are powerless because they have replaced discernment with diagnosis, and deliverance with dialogue. Enough!

Jesus never turned anyone away. But He also never ignored a demon. He rebuked the unclean spirits. He commanded healing. He ministered to the soul and the spirit. That's the model. That's the way forward.

This book is for anyone who has ever been to the edge. Anyone who has ever felt so overwhelmed that death seemed like relief. Anyone who has stood at the casket of a loved one and wondered what really happened. Anyone who is tired of religious answers and looking for spiritual power.

Before you say goodbye, give God a chance to speak. Before you say goodbye, open your heart to truth. Before you say goodbye, let someone fight with you.

You are not alone.

You are loved.

You are chosen.

PART I

THE INVISISBLE WAR BEHIND SUICIDAL ASSAULTS

CHAPTER 1

SUICIDE IS NOT THE END

The thief comes only to steal and kill and destroy. I came that they may have life and have it abundantly.".
John 10:10

BREAKING SUICIDAL THOUGHTS

When a person is drowning in hopelessness, the thought of suicide can begin to sound like an invitation to rest. It rarely comes with the violence of a shout; it begins with a whisper that promises peace. The voice says, "You'll finally be free. No more pain, no more shame, no more weight to carry." Those words often sound compassionate, like an understanding friend who just wants your suffering to end. Yet, behind that whisper hides a dark intelligence. Those words are not mercy; they are manipulation. They are the subtle voice of the same thief Jesus warned about, the one whose only purpose is to steal, to kill, and to destroy.

Suicide dresses itself as an escape, but escape to where? That question changes everything. What many never stop to consider is that suicide does not end the story; it changes the setting. You do not simply vanish into nothingness. The body dies, but the soul continues. You enter a realm more real, more permanent, and far more consequential than this one. The enemy's plan is not to free you from pain, but to ensure you never experience peace. His goal is to end your earthly suffering only so he can begin your eternal torment.

Jesus, on the other hand, never offered escape through death. He offered life through Himself. When the darkness tells you that death is the only way to end pain, remember that Christ already entered death and defeated it, so that you would never have to face it alone or in despair.

The Moment You Step Through the Door

Every culture, ancient or modern, has believed in some form of afterlife because the human heart knows instinctively that we were not made to end in dust. Ecclesiastes 3:11 says that God "has set eternity in the human heart." We are wired for forever. Death is not a wall; it is a doorway. And once you cross it, the door never swings back.

When the body dies, the soul passes into an eternal reality. What you meet there depends entirely on whom you belong to. Some imagine death as a peaceful blank space, a dreamless void where all suffering stops. That illusion is one of hell's most effective lies. In Luke 16, Jesus told the story of a rich man who died and immediately found himself in torment. He was conscious, aware, and full of regret. He could remember his life and recognize the choices that led him there. He begged for relief, but none came. Death didn't erase his awareness; it magnified it.

This is the truth no one wants to face: death is not the end. It is the continuation of what you lived for. The life you live now determines what eternity will look like later.

When a person chooses suicide, they are not trying to end their existence, they are trying to end their pain. They are running from unbearable emotional torment, relentless mental anguish, or memories that replay like open wounds. Those experiences are real. They hurt deeply. They can make every day feel like punishment. But they are also temporary. Pain is a season; it is not forever.

Suicide, however, is a permanent reaction to a temporary condition. It offers an illusion of control, a way to make the suffering stop on your own terms. But what you're really doing is forfeiting your chance for God to intervene. You are not escaping suffering; you are surrendering the possibility of healing. You are not leaving behind your chaos; you are abandoning your opportunity for peace. Jesus stands ready to redeem even the darkest pain, but suicide cuts short the story before redemption can unfold.

The enemy never tells you that part. He never shows you what you'll lose, only what you think you'll escape.

BREAKING SUICIDAL THOUGHTS

Jesus drew the contrast clearly: "The thief comes only to steal and kill and destroy. I came that they may have life." (John 10:10) The thief's strategy is deception. He does not need to drag you into sin with force; he only needs to convince you to walk willingly toward destruction. He paints despair as relief and death as freedom. He whispers half-truths that sound compassionate but carry poison beneath the surface.

He will never show you the aftermath of suicide, the grief of your family, the emptiness in those who loved you, the eternal consequences of a life cut short without reconciliation. He shows only one image: false peace. It is a mirage. What he truly seeks is your eternal separation from God.

Christ, by contrast, offers abundant life, not the absence of pain, but the presence of His peace in the midst of it. The difference between the thief and the Shepherd is this: one takes your life to destroy it; the other gives His life to redeem yours.

Pain is real. Christians are not immune to it, and pretending otherwise only deepens despair. People do not think of suicide because they are weak or selfish; they think of it because they are exhausted, desperate, and unable to see a way out. In those dark moments, the mind repeats phrases like, "I'll never get better," or "Nothing will ever change." Those thoughts echo like prophecy, convincing the sufferer that tomorrow will mirror today forever.

But those thoughts are not truth, they are interpretations filtered through pain. They are lies birthed in the darkness of despair. The Word of God confronts that illusion directly: "For everything there is a season, and a time for every purpose under heaven." (Ecclesiastes 3:1) That includes the season you are in right now.

Suffering feels eternal while it lasts, but it has an expiration date. What feels permanent is often just prolonged. Many who once contemplated suicide are now living testimonies of transformation. The difference was not that their pain instantly vanished, but that they waited long enough for change to come. They refused to make an eternal decision in a temporary storm.

If you can outlast the storm, you will see the sunrise.

Eternal Life Doesn't End

The human soul is immortal. Whether you believe it or not, eternity is already written into your being. This short life is just a blink compared to forever. When someone ends their own life, they are trading a temporary suffering for an everlasting consequence. If a person dies outside of Christ, the suffering does not stop, it intensifies, and there is no relief.

Jesus came to prevent exactly that. He came to offer not only eternal life in the world to come but abundant life in the present world. That abundance doesn't mean a life free of pain. It means a life anchored by hope, steadied by purpose, and infused with supernatural strength that transcends circumstances.

Jesus Himself suffered deeply. He knew the weight of sorrow, betrayal, and rejection. He cried, He sweated blood, He felt forsaken. Yet He endured because He saw what was beyond the pain, resurrection, redemption, and restoration. Your suffering, too, can be a passage to resurrection. The pain you carry is not proof that God has abandoned you; it may be evidence that He is preparing something new through you.

BREAKING SUICIDAL THOUGHTS

Accounts from those who have experienced near-death encounters are remarkably consistent. Many describe instant awareness the moment they left their bodies. Some found themselves surrounded by an overwhelming presence of light and love. Others encountered terrifying darkness. The veil between worlds is thin, and death pulls it back. These are not mere hallucinations; they are glimpses into the spiritual reality that surrounds us even now.

A person who attempted suicide once described their experience: "The moment I died, I realized it wasn't over, it had just begun. I begged God to let me return." Some are given that mercy. Most are not. This is what makes suicide spiritually deadly, not just because it ends a physical life, but because it may finalize a soul's separation from God.

There are no redos after death. Once the door closes, the story written in time becomes the story sealed in eternity.

If the enemy can isolate you, he can influence you. Like a predator hunting a wounded animal that has strayed from the herd, the devil targets those who feel cut off from others. He whispers, "No one understands you. No one cares. You're all alone." Those lies build emotional walls that separate you from the very people God sent to help you heal.

Isolation is not merely being physically alone; it is the internal decision to hide your pain. It is shame's best friend and despair's perfect environment. In that isolation, darkness grows. Yet the Bible commands us to live differently: "Bear one another's burdens, and so fulfill the law of Christ." (Galatians 6:2) God designed community to protect us from the lies that thrive in solitude.

If your mind tells you to withdraw, to stop answering calls, or to avoid help, pause and ask yourself, Where is this voice coming from?

God's voice leads you toward life and relationship. The enemy's voice leads you toward secrecy and silence. When you step back into connection, even if only with one safe person, light begins to break the darkness.

Despair is not just a feeling of sadness; it is the absence of hope. It is a slow, invisible poison that drains life from the soul and blinds the heart to the possibility of change. Despair doesn't begin as a storm, it begins as a fog, soft and silent, until you can't see your way forward. It tells you that nothing will ever get better, that you are cursed to suffer, and that tomorrow will only bring more pain. It says, "You've tried everything. Nothing works. Just give up."

But despair is not merely psychological, it is spiritual. Isaiah 61:3 identifies it clearly as "the spirit of heaviness." Many people battling suicidal thoughts describe the sensation of being crushed beneath an invisible weight. They wake up exhausted, even after sleep. Their mind feels clouded, their chest tight. They say it feels like darkness is sitting on them. That's because this is not just emotion, it is warfare.

Satan's tactic is to convince you that the fog is the truth. He uses feelings to distort reality. He wants you to mistake the heaviness of the spirit realm for evidence that God has left you. But feelings are not facts. Despair tells you you're abandoned, but Scripture tells you the opposite. Psalm 34:18 declares that "The Lord is close to the brokenhearted and saves those who are crushed in spirit." The very presence of that crushing pain is proof that God is near, not absent.

Despair thrives in secrecy, but it begins to die when you name it. When you confess your hopelessness to God and to a trusted believer, the fog starts to lift. Truth breaks the spell of lies, and the soul begins to breathe again.

BREAKING SUICIDAL THOUGHTS

The Strategy of Subtlety

The enemy almost never begins with open destruction. He begins with whispers. The thoughts he plants are often small, seemingly harmless, but they are designed to multiply. The person who ends their life rarely moves from joy to despair overnight, it's a gradual descent that begins with subtle lies such as, "You're a burden," or "No one would really miss you," These thoughts may sound like your own, but they are seeds from an ancient deceiver who knows the power of suggestion.

At first, these thoughts may seem like fleeting emotions, but once repeated, they start to feel like truth. The longer you agree with them, the deeper their roots grow. Eventually, they become strongholds, mental fortresses that seem unbreakable. That's why Scripture commands believers to "take every thought captive to obey Christ" (2 Corinthians 10:5). The battle is won or lost in the mind.

When a lie is not confronted, it becomes a lens. You begin to see yourself, your circumstances, and even God through it. The whisper becomes your worldview. And when you accept the lie as truth, your emotions and decisions follow. But the Word of God exposes the enemy's subtlety. It reveals that your life has worth, that you are loved, and that your pain is not purposeless. The moment you confront the lie with truth, its power begins to break.

That's why filling your mind with Scripture, worship, and godly counsel isn't religious duty, it's spiritual defense. Light has to be fed daily, or darkness will creep back in.

There are those whose suffering comes not from ordinary disappointment but from deep trauma. Abuse, abandonment, betrayal, and chronic rejection can fracture the soul. The memories linger like ghosts that refuse to leave. These experiences shape how we interpret reality. For the traumatized person, love feels unsafe, hope feels naive, and trust feels impossible.

The enemy does not always create these wounds, but he exploits them masterfully. He slips into the cracks of the human heart and uses trauma as evidence against God. He reminds you of what happened, accuses you of being unworthy, and whispers that you are beyond repair. He turns pain into a prison and convinces you that suicide is the only key to freedom.

But Jesus holds a different key. His mission in Isaiah 61:1. 3 was to "bind up the brokenhearted" and to "give beauty for ashes, the oil of joy for mourning." He doesn't just forgive sins; He heals wounds. He doesn't simply save souls; He restores lives. He enters the places where the enemy has whispered lies and speaks truth louder.

When trauma is brought into the presence of Jesus, it begins to lose its authority. The memories may remain, but their power to define you breaks. Healing doesn't erase your story; it rewrites its ending. The abuse, the rejection, and the pain that once fueled despair can become the testimony that fuels deliverance for others.

You are not damaged beyond repair. You are the very kind of person Jesus came for, the crushed, the weary, the ones who have lost the will to live. In His hands, the shattered become sacred.

One of the reasons Satan attacks with such intensity is because he sees what you cannot yet see: your potential. He knows the weight of your calling and the impact you could have if you ever walk fully in your identity in Christ. Before you even recognize your own destiny, the enemy recognizes it.

That's why the attacks often start early. He works through pain, through rejection, through words spoken over you, to destroy your confidence before you discover your purpose. He knows that if you live long enough to encounter the truth of who you are in God, you will become a weapon against his kingdom. So, he wages war to make you self-destruct before you awaken.

But if you are reading this, it means the thief has not won. His lies have not consumed you. You are still breathing, and that means there is still purpose in your lungs. The very fact that you've survived what should have killed you is evidence of divine preservation. The storm didn't take you because your story isn't finished.

Satan wanted your destruction because he feared your destiny. But God is rewriting the script. You were never meant to die in despair, you were meant to live to display His glory.

When Jesus said, "I have come that they may have life, and have it abundantly," He wasn't describing a life without hardship. He was promising a life overflowing with divine presence and eternal meaning. The abundant life is not the absence of pain; it is the awareness of God within it.

Abundant life means walking through fire without being consumed, standing in storms without being swept away, and finding peace that defies explanation. It means discovering joy not because circumstances are perfect, but because His presence is constant.

Jesus does not offer fantasy escape. He offers transformation. He doesn't erase every scar; He turns scars into testimonies. He doesn't always remove the valley, but He walks through it beside you. Abundant life begins the moment you exchange your self-sufficiency for His sufficiency, your despair for His hope, and your death wish for His resurrection power.

When Jesus enters a life, even the darkest corners fill with light. He restores what the enemy has stolen. He resurrects the dreams buried beneath disappointment. He whispers, "Behold, I make all things new." (Revelation 21:5) That includes you, your mind, your emotions, your story.

Many believe they've crossed the point of no return, that they've failed too deeply, sinned too greatly, or broken too completely for God to care. But grace was made for that very place. Jesus doesn't meet you at the finish line of perfection; He meets you in the rubble of despair. He steps into your darkness, sits beside you, and offers His hand.

Psalm 34:18 says, "The Lord is close to the brokenhearted and saves those who are crushed in spirit." That means you, right now, in your current state. You are not too far gone. The very breath you're taking as you read these words is proof that hope still exists.

When God says He will never leave nor forsake you, He means it. Even in the silence, He is near. Even when you feel unworthy, His love is unchanged. He promises, "When you pass through the waters, I will be with you... when you walk through the fire, you will not be burned." (Isaiah 43:2)

His deliverance may not come in the form you expect, but it will come. Sometimes His rescue is not removing you from the pain, it's walking with you until the pain turns to power.

Despair tells you that death is the only release. Jesus tells you that life can still be redeemed. He offers not survival, but restoration, not endurance, but renewal. When He says, "Come to me, all you who are weary and burdened, and I will give you rest," (Matthew 11:28) He is not speaking metaphorically. He is offering Himself. Rest is not a state of mind, it's a person.

And that person is Jesus.

Reflection Questions

Use these questions for journaling, prayer, or conversation with a trusted friend, pastor, or counselor. Be honest. Healing begins with truth.

1. Have you ever believed the lie that suicide would end your pain? Where do you think that belief came from, your own thoughts, your experiences, or outside influences?

2. What are the emotions or circumstances that make you feel isolated or forgotten? Can you identify specific moments or memories that have contributed to those feelings?

3. What has despair tried to tell you about your future? What does God say about your future in His Word? Look up scriptures like Jeremiah 29:11 and Psalm 23.

4. Do you struggle with seeing your life as valuable or purposeful? Why do you think that is? Have you allowed your past or pain to define your worth?

5. Are you willing to let Jesus enter into your suffering, even if your situation doesn't immediately change? What might it look like to walk with Him daily, one step at a time?

Key Takeaways

- Suicide is not the end, it is a transition into eternity. Ending your physical life does not erase your pain but potentially amplifies it in the spiritual realm.
- The enemy of your soul uses lies, isolation, and despair to push you toward self-destruction. His mission is to steal, kill, and destroy (John 10:10).
- The pain you feel today is real, but it is also temporary. Suffering is seasonal; eternity is forever.
- God offers not just survival, but abundant life, peace, healing, and purpose through a relationship with Jesus Christ.
- You are not alone. God is near to the brokenhearted and saves those crushed in spirit (Psalm 34:18).
- Your thoughts and feelings, while powerful, are not always truthful. God's Word is the standard of truth and hope.
- There is still purpose for your life. As long as you are alive, God can redeem your story and use it to bring light to others.
- Healing starts when you expose the lies and allow God's truth to shape your mind, identity, and future.

CHAPTER 2

THE VOICE THAT WHISPERS DEATH

"When he lies, he speaks his native language, for he is a liar and the father of lies.". John 8:44

BREAKING SUICIDAL THOUGHTS

"You should just end it." "They'd be better off without you." "No one really cares." Those whispers arrive in the empty places, moments of weakness, grief, or prolonged despair, and because they are tuned to your pain, they often sound like your own thinking.

But listen closely: these are not your thoughts; they are the carefully disguised lies of an enemy who studies the human wound and knows how to speak into it. Satan's craft is impersonation. He does not arrive with a mask that makes him obvious; he weaves falsehood into the fabric of your interior speech, copying your tone, replaying your deepest regrets, and exploiting familiar vulnerabilities until the lie feels convincing.

His goal is simple and brutal: to make you believe that the most self-destructive thoughts are your own reasoning. Scripture calls him a liar and the father of lies, and every time you hear a voice urging disconnection, you are hearing the echo of that ancient strategy, not the voice of truth.

The Power of Suggestion

Suicidal thoughts seldom begin as violent storms; they start as a drop of poison in the well. They enter quietly after loss, after rejection, after nights of lonely thinking. The first whisper is the seed: "Why do I even try?" "Maybe things would be better if I weren't here." "No one would notice if I disappeared."

The enemy operates in layers. He plants the seed of an idea and returns later to water it with fatigue, loneliness, and resentment. He times his suggestions when your defenses are weakest, when you are emotionally raw or spiritually distant, and then he watches to see if you nurture the lie. If you replay the phrase, it becomes familiar. If you accept it as a stray thought, it will root.

The tactic is methodical: use the moment of vulnerability, offer a seeming relief, and wait for you to consent. That is how the vine grows until hopelessness strangles the life from the soul.

Satan's approach has always been the same: twist, quote, and wait. Look at Matthew 4, where he tempted Jesus after a season of fasting. He did not invent new lies; he twisted truth and quoted Scripture back at the Son. He waited until hunger and fatigue dulled judgment, then offered a plausible distortion.

That is his method still, finding the moment when need and weakness meet and then whispering a counterfeit option. He will whisper, "If you were really loved, wouldn't someone have reached out by now?" or "If God was real, why did He allow this?" or "If you matter, why do you feel invisible?" He crafts his lies to press where you are raw and to make God look distant. The strategy is not original; it is a replay of the same ancient attack, and it preys on the timing of your frailty.

It's crucial to understand that not every thought that sounds personal is generated by you. The apostle Paul reminds us in Ephesians 6:12 that our struggle is not primarily against people but against spiritual forces, principalities, and rulers of darkness. Some thoughts are planted, not born.

The enemy customizes his lies to the wounds he finds; if you were raised without affirmation, his voice will target worthiness; if you know rejection, he will replay abandonment; if trauma marks your history, he will mimic hopelessness. Because the lies sound tailored, they often feel true. But feeling true does not equal being true. The origin matters. When a thought arrives with accusation, finality, or isolation, suspect its origin.

Learning to distinguish your voice from the enemy's requires a few markers. The enemy's voice primarily condemns; it speaks in absolutes. "You're worthless," "You'll never change," "You might as well give up."

God's voice, by contrast, convicts with tenderness and calls toward restoration: "Come home," "You are loved," "There is hope." The enemy's speech isolates; it pushes you away from people, from community, and even from God. The Lord's voice draws you toward relationship and healing.

The enemy's tone is urgent, chaotic, and demanding immediate action, especially destructive action. God's voice brings a steady peace, even when correction is needed. Where the enemy distorts identity, saying you are your failures or trauma. God's voice reorients identity toward truth: you are fearfully and wonderfully made, a treasured child of the Creator, not reducible to your worst moment. These differences are not academic; they are lifelines for the desperate.

When you can name the whisper as a lie, you begin to dismantle its power. Darkness flourishes in secrecy and anonymity; truth thrives in sunlight. It is not enough to feel resistance toward destructive thoughts; you must speak back. If the enemy whispers "You are unloved," respond aloud, "God loves me with an everlasting love." If the lie says "You're a burden," say, "I am God's beloved."

The battle is not fought by matching thought-for-thought; it is won by confronting lies with Scripture and declaring what is true.

Speaking truth aloud engages your will and enlists heaven's authority against the deception. The act of naming is itself an eviction notice to the lie.

The Path from Thought to Stronghold

Thoughts are small, but they are seeds that shape destiny. A single destructive thought left unchecked becomes a rehearsed refrain. Rehearsal hardens into identity; identity drives choices.

A suicidal idea is not merely a passing feeling; it can be the opening move in a calculated progression that converts suggestion into spiritual stronghold.

The enemy cannot simply force a person to end their life; he builds a pattern that moves from idea to habit to identity and then to action. Once belief has formed a foundation, the mind reads the world through that belief. What follows looks less like external coercion and more like internal inevitability. That's the danger, what was once foreign becomes intimate and then indistinguishable from "who I am."

The blueprint of destruction is steady and intentional. First, a lie is whispered: "You're a failure," "You don't matter," "There's no way out." If the lie is entertained, it is rehearsed, played over in private moments until it feels familiar.

Familiarity breeds acceptance, and acceptance hardens into identity: "I'm a failure," "I'm hopeless." Finally, identity drives action: isolation becomes habit, despair dictates decisions, and dangerous choices feel like reasonable responses.

BREAKING SUICIDAL THOUGHTS

The demon's work in the mind resembles a builder laying one brick at a time: introduce the idea, encourage the repetition, normalize the identity, and then capitalize on action. Without intervention, the structure becomes a fortress against truth.

A stronghold is a spiritual structure in the mind composed of lies, emotions, memories, and repeated assumptions. Paul speaks of demolishing arguments and pretensions that set themselves up against the knowledge of God, and that demolition begins by recognizing the fortress for what it is: not reality but an architecture of deceit.

To those who live inside a stronghold it feels like home; to God it is an enemy's camp that must be taken apart. The stronghold persuades your heart that the lie is self-evident. But strongholds are not invincible; they have foundations, repetition, reinforcement, isolation, and inner vows, that can be exposed and removed.

Repetition is the mortar of the stronghold. The more you rehearse a lie it becomes a reflex, and reflexes shape identity.

Emotional reinforcement, trauma, rejection, or repeated failure, acts as "evidence" to the lie and convinces the mind that the narrative is true.

Isolation starves out contradiction; when no one hears your internal dialogue, no one can challenge the lie. Inner vows, subconscious agreements like "I'll never trust again" or "I don't deserve to live", become chains.

Trauma is often the soil in which these structures take root: childhood rejection opens the door to unlovability; repetitive failure strengthens worthlessness; grief can convince you joy is impossible.

The enemy reuses the same access points because they work. Yet none of this is permanent; knowing how the stronghold was built gives you the keys to dismantle it.

Trauma does not merely sit in memory; it fractures perception. When a person has been abused, abandoned, bullied, or betrayed, the wound creates an opening, an index of truth that the enemy can exploit. He does not need to invent a new lie; he repurposes the old wound as evidence. He then invites the wounded person to accept a new identity based on that trauma.

But Jesus specializes in entering those broken places. He binds up the brokenhearted and turns ashes into beauty. Trauma shapes the narrative but does not have to dictate the ending. When trauma is exposed to the light of God's presence, its authority to define you is stripped away.

Discerning the Voice of God in the Noise

In the chaos of competing voices, God's speech always leans toward life. The enemy's words bend toward death, death of joy, hope, identity, and ultimately life. God's words bring restoration: where the enemy says "You've messed up beyond repair,"

Scripture offers mercy and cleansing; where the liar insists you are unloved, the Lord declares everlasting love; where the whisper urges an end, Jesus declares an abundant life. God's voice corrects without destroying; it draws near without driving away. It is patient, still, and rooted in love, even when it confronts.

Silencing the enemy begins by silencing the other voices that amplify him: toxic media, bitter conversations, and the internal monologue that repeats lies on loop. Create space for truth, read

Scripture aloud, sing worship that invites God's presence, and let biblical words be louder than your thoughts. Speak truth even when you do not feel it; declarations of God's character are administered as medicine until your spirit aligns with reality. Invite someone in, confession and honest community expose the lie to light and begin the healing process. And pray with brutal honesty; scream if you must. God is not afraid of your pain; He meets you in the rawness and draws closest where your voice is loudest with need.

Freedom begins with recognition. Identify where the enemy has entered, unhealed trauma, unforgiveness, repeated agreement with death-minded phrases, or occult exposure.

Repentance is more than remorse; it is a reversal of allegiance, a deliberate breaking of agreements with lies and a replacement of those agreements with truth. Invite the Holy Spirit to fill the places the lie occupied, for if the house is left empty the enemy can return.

Replace the lie with Scripture and daily declarations: remind yourself you are fearfully and wonderfully made, that God is with you, that there is a future and a hope.

Establish new patterns, connect with a Spirit-led community, guard the media you consume, speak life into your situation, and serve others to displace inward collapse with outward purpose. These are not magic formulas; they are the spiritual strategy the Scriptures give to demolish strongholds and rebuild minds on the foundation of Christ.

Behind every recurring suicidal or self-destructive thought is a spiritual intelligence that studies emotional cycles, observing when the heart is most vulnerable. The enemy waits for patterns, moments of loss, shame, or fatigue, and returns to exploit them. This is not random; it is targeted warfare.

The spirit of death does not attack only through external events but through internal dialogue. It hijacks language, converts pain into prophecy, and then turns suggestion into self-hate. It whispers not merely to end a life but to end purpose.

The war is not about your breath, it is about your assignment. If the enemy cannot stop your salvation, he will try to terminate your usefulness. That is why suicide often follows seasons of divine calling; hell reacts to destiny.

The spirit of death is not just a demon that kills; it is a philosophy that persuades. It promises relief without redemption. It tells the weary, "Sleep forever and you will be free." But the truth is this: suicide does not end suffering, it transfers it.

The pain you attempt to silence becomes generational, echoing through those left behind. The enemy knows this, and his cruelty is deliberate. He seeks to multiply grief through one act of deception. But Christ came to destroy the works of the devil, not only by breaking visible chains but by reclaiming inner conversations.

When the Spirit of Christ dwells within, He begins to filter thought, revealing when an idea does not belong. The anointing teaches discernment by peace, peace becomes the indicator of truth, and disturbance becomes the signal of deception.

BREAKING SUICIDAL THOUGHTS

When the Voice Sounds Compassionate

Many imagine demonic whispers as loud and terrifying, but the more dangerous ones often sound compassionate. The thought may arrive clothed in empathy: "You've been through too much," "You deserve rest," "No one understands what you carry." These sound comforting but are traps.

The spirit of death masquerades as comforter because it cannot force destruction, it must convince you that destruction is mercy. But the Holy Spirit is the true Comforter. He never leads toward death; He leads toward restoration.

The counterfeit comfort of the enemy is temporary anesthesia that leads to eternal damage. The authentic comfort of the Spirit brings healing that leads to life.

Discernment grows when believers test the spirit of comfort behind their thoughts. The enemy's compassion isolates; God's compassion integrates. The enemy's comfort leads you to secrecy; God's comfort draws you to confession.

The enemy's whisper glorifies escape; God's whisper offers endurance. If the voice you hear suggests that your life is expendable, know this, it is not the voice of the Shepherd. The Shepherd lays down His life for the sheep; He never asks the sheep to destroy themselves.

No spirit has authority without human agreement. The enemy can suggest, but he cannot enforce. Every victory of darkness requires consent, spoken, emotional, or behavioral.

Agreement is not always verbal; sometimes it is silent resignation, the internal nod that says, "Maybe that's true." That single nod becomes the seed of partnership. Once you agree, even unconsciously, the voice grows louder because it now echoes inside the chamber of your own belief. Agreement is the power line through which demonic influence flows.

Breaking the power of suicidal thought, therefore, begins with breaking agreement. It requires renouncing every word, vow, or inner verdict that has aligned with death. That is why repentance is not shame, it is liberation.

When you renounce lies, you cut the power cord connecting darkness to your identity. Speak it aloud: "I break agreement with the spirit of death. I align my mind with the Spirit of Life in Christ Jesus." The spoken word carries authority; silence concedes ground. Hell is not afraid of thoughts, it fears declarations of truth.

God redeems even the darkest mental battles by turning them into prophetic ministries. Those who once heard the voice of death can become instruments of deliverance for others. Your survival becomes intercession. Your healing becomes a weapon. Every scar becomes a sermon of hope.

The enemy attacks what threatens him most; if he targeted your mind with self-destruction, it is because your voice carries deliverance for others bound in despair. What once whispered death will one day tremble when you speak life.

The devil never attacks potential that is useless to him; he fights what carries divine voltage. You were not born to die prematurely; you were born to be a living proof that darkness does not win.

The greatest antidote to the voice of death is the written Word of God. The Scriptures are not inspirational poetry; they are living weapons. Jesus did not argue with Satan in the wilderness. He responded with "It is written." The power was not in discussion but in declaration.

The believer who memorizes and declares Scripture fortifies the mind against deception. Verses like Psalm 118:17, "I shall not die, but live, and declare the works of the Lord," act as shields. When repeated in faith, they restructure thought pathways, breaking demonic patterns. The Word not only silences lies but rewires the mind toward truth.

In the spiritual world, words create atmosphere. If you live under constant mental assault, saturate your environment with Scripture. Speak the Word in your room, write it on mirrors, play it in worship. Let your house echo with truth until the frequency of heaven overrules the static of hell. It is impossible for a mind filled with truth to remain captive to lies. The Word dismantles strongholds by reprogramming the inner dialogue that once served darkness.

Community and Confession

Isolation is the devil's ally. Silence is the incubator of deception. Healing begins in confession, first to God, then to trusted people. James 5:16 says, "Confess your faults one to another and pray for one another, that you may be healed." Notice the sequence: confession and prayer bring healing. You may have prayed alone for deliverance, but healing is often locked in relational confession. When light enters, shame loses power. The moment you voice your hidden battle, you break secrecy, and secrecy is the oxygen of the demonic.

Community restores perspective.

When others speak truth over your mind, they become mirrors reflecting reality you cannot see in yourself. The Church must become the safest place for confession, not a courtroom but a hospital. Spiritual families that carry intercessory power can stand in the gap, renounce the spirit of death corporately, and surround the wounded with worship and Word. You do not conquer inner voices by isolation; you conquer them in communion.

Romans 8:2 declares, "The law of the Spirit of life in Christ Jesus has set me free from the law of sin and death." This is not metaphor; it is legal language. There are spiritual laws, sin and death on one side, life in Christ on the other.

When you align your belief with the Spirit of Life, you are no longer bound by the law of death. That means suicidal compulsion, addiction, and despair lose jurisdiction. You can decree it: "I am under the law of life. Death has no legal claim on me." This is not denial; it is divine legislation. Faith activates jurisdictional transfer, out of the kingdom of darkness into the kingdom of light.

Every day, declare your citizenship. You belong to the realm of life, not death. The more you rehearse that truth, the more your atmosphere shifts. Angels respond to spoken Word, not to silent wishes. Heaven enforces declarations of truth, and the Spirit empowers what you confess. Life is not just a gift; it is an assignment. Guard it fiercely.

Hope is not naïve optimism; it is spiritual defiance. It is the refusal to allow darkness the final word. Hope says, "I don't feel strong, but I believe God is not done." It is the most subversive act against despair. When you choose hope, you announce to hell that its narrative has failed. That single decision shifts atmospheres, because hope invites the presence of God. He inhabits not only praise but expectation. Every time you expect His goodness, you create a portal for His intervention.

Even if your emotions are numb, choose to hope. Hope is not emotion; it is decision. It is the anchor that prevents drift when storms rage. When hope lives, faith breathes, and when faith breathes, miracles begin. The enemy's ultimate agenda is not suicide, it is hopelessness. If he can suffocate hope, death becomes appealing. But when hope rises, death loses its argument.

Reflection Questions

1. What are the specific thoughts or phrases that often sound like your own voice but carry the tone of despair or finality?

2. How can you discern whether a "comforting" thought is truly from the Holy Spirit or a counterfeit voice of death?

3. Have you identified areas in your life where silent agreement with lies may have given the enemy a foothold?

4. In what ways can confession and community act as spiritual weapons in restoring mental strength?

5. How does Romans 8:2 change your understanding of spiritual authority over destructive thoughts?

6. What prophetic assignment might your survival be pointing to?

7. How can you practically cultivate hope daily, even when emotions feel numb or faith feels distant?

Key Takeaways

- The voice of death often imitates compassion to gain agreement, but its intent is destruction, not comfort.
- The enemy requires human consent to influence; breaking agreement dismantles his access.
- The Spirit of Life in Christ legally overrides the power of death for those who believe.
- Hope is an act of resistance; it keeps the atmosphere open for God's intervention.
- Every survivor of suicidal battle carries prophetic authority to set others free.

CHAPTER 3

THE SPIRIT BEHIND SUICIDE

For God has not given us a spirit of fear, but of power, and of love, and of a sound mind.". 2 Timothy 1:7

BREAKING SUICIDAL THOUGHTS

The spirit behind suicide is not merely a human emotion of despair, it is an intelligent and malevolent force. It works slowly, often beginning in moments of deep pain or trauma. Like a parasite, it feeds on rejection, abandonment, and grief. It waits until the soul is wounded enough to listen. It speaks in first person. "I want to die," "I can't take this anymore", so the victim believes the voice is their own.

But God's Word is clear: He has not given us a spirit of fear, but of power, love, and a sound mind. If what you are hearing leads you to fear, confusion, hopelessness, or death, it is not from God. There is a difference between a thought and a spiritual assault.

The spirit of suicide is patient. It isolates. It pushes you to withdraw from friends, stop praying, stop hoping. It lies to you: "They won't understand," "You'll ruin the mood if you talk," "Just smile and act fine." As isolation deepens, so does agreement with the voice.

What most don't realize is that agreement with the lie gives it power. When you begin to repeat those thoughts, you give spiritual permission for the enemy to fortify his presence in your mind. What began as a whisper becomes a stronghold.

No one wants to die without a reason. Suicide is always connected to a deep desire to escape pain, whether it's emotional, physical, relational, or mental. But pain in itself is not evil. It's a signal, like fire to the skin, pain alerts us that something is wrong. The enemy twists this signal. He whispers, "The pain won't stop, unless you die."

In reality, the pain is calling you toward healing, not destruction. But healing requires vulnerability, time, and support, three things the spirit of suicide wants to cut you off from. That's why it attacks your trust, your hope, and your sense of being loved.

The demonic voice of suicide often cloaks itself in logic. It says, "You've failed too much. You're just sparing everyone. You've tried everything already." But demonic logic always has one common result: death. The final destination of its reasoning is always your removal from this life. It doesn't account for grace, healing, or the future God still has for you. Its arguments are structured to appear rational, even noble, but they are built on lies and finality.

If your thoughts are pressuring you to give up completely, stop and examine their origin. Would a God of love and healing lead you into death, especially through despair? Never.

Why the Enemy Wants You Dead

Suicide is not just about escaping pain, it is a spiritual robbery. The enemy fears who you might become if you survive this season. He knows there is an assignment over your life. He knows that healing is possible, that restoration is near. So he pushes for an early exit.

Imagine someone cutting down a tree that hasn't yet borne fruit. That's what the enemy is trying to do with you. He doesn't want to deal with your testimony, your healing, your influence, your voice. Suicide isn't random, it is targeted spiritual warfare.

But here's the truth: if hell is working this hard to destroy you, heaven must have a mighty plan for you. You are not being attacked because you're worthless. You're being attacked because you're valuable.

This isn't just a matter of mental health, it's a matter of spiritual truth and authority. Yes, therapy helps. Yes, community matters. Yes, medication may bring balance. But beyond all these, you must also learn to take authority over spiritual voices that do not belong in your mind.

You must rise up and say: "I renounce the spirit of suicide in Jesus' name." "I reject the lie that I am worthless." "I receive God's love and sound mind." "I will live and not die, and declare the works of the Lord." (Psalm 118:17)

This kind of spiritual confrontation is not optional, it's essential. You must fight for your mind, and you must fight for your life.

To many, death seems like the final curtain, a vanishing into nothingness. But Scripture and countless testimonies confirm the opposite: death is not the end, it is a transition. And that transition is far more spiritual than most people realize.

When someone dies, whether through natural causes or suicide, their spirit separates from the physical body. In the Bible, James 2:26 tells us, "the body without the spirit is dead." This separation is not a fading into unconsciousness but a full spiritual awakening. You do not cease to be; you become more acutely aware.

Those who have had near-death experiences often report heightened senses, complete awareness, and full recall of events that happened around them, even from outside their bodies. That's because the soul is still very much alive. It can see, hear, feel, and think, perhaps even more clearly than before. Emotions, memory, and spiritual perception continue. There is no "off switch."

The Spirit Behind Suicide

The moment the spirit leaves the body, it enters a spiritual realm. And which realm it enters depends not on how the person died but on whom they lived for.

Hebrews 9:27 says, "It is appointed for man to die once, and after that comes judgment." There is no pause, no reset button, no time-out. Immediately after death, a person's soul is ushered into the spiritual consequence of their earthly choices.

If they died in Christ, trusting Him as Lord and Savior, their soul is received by God's angels and brought into His presence. Luke 16:22 describes how the angels carried Lazarus into Abraham's bosom (a reference to paradise). But if they died in rebellion, rejecting God's mercy, the soul descends into darkness, into torment, like the rich man in the same parable, who "being in torment, lifted up his eyes" in Hades (Luke 16:23).

This judgment isn't about whether someone lived a perfect life, but whether they accepted or rejected God's grace through Jesus.

Now here's the sobering truth: suicide doesn't end pain, it may begin eternal pain. The moment someone dies by suicide, they are not led into peace unless they belonged to Christ. Instead of escaping darkness, many fall straight into the very torment they were trying to avoid. The same demon that whispered, "End it," now turns to accuse and torment them in the spirit realm.

Suicide, for those outside of Christ, is a spiritual ambush, a trap disguised as relief.

Even for believers, suicide is a dangerous and tragic mistake. While salvation is a gift that cannot be earned, Scripture never guarantees what happens to someone who dies in a moment of despair and rebellion. God is merciful, but He is also just, and only He knows the true state of each heart at death. That's why no one should ever presume grace as a safety net for self-destruction.

Demonic Escort at Death

Just as angels escort the righteous into the presence of God, demons escort the wicked. Many who have survived suicide attempts or near-death experiences describe a terrifying presence that tried to pull them down. These were not hallucinations. They were spiritual beings, present at the boundary between life and death.

The spirit of suicide is not finished with a person once they die, it seeks to claim that soul. Hell is not just a place, it's a kingdom with laws and jurisdictions. If a person dies under the authority of a demonic spirit, through deception, agreement, and rebellion against God, they may find themselves immediately subjected to that authority on the other side.

This is why you must never treat suicidal thoughts as harmless or purely emotional. There is a spiritual battle taking place over your soul, and the enemy fights hardest when he knows your destiny is valuable.

This is not meant to scare you into submission but to awaken you to reality. If you are struggling with suicidal thoughts right now, you are under attack, but you are not hopeless.

You are not your thoughts.
You are not your pain.
You are not beyond help.
You are not beyond grace.

Jesus said, "The thief comes only to steal and kill and destroy. I came that they may have life and have it abundantly." (John 10:10)

Life is still possible. Healing is still available. The darkness may be loud, but it is not all-powerful. There is One greater who stands ready to rescue, restore, and defend you, if you will call on Him.

The Three-Part Human: Spirit, Soul, and Body

To understand what truly happens when someone dies, or more specifically, when someone dies by suicide, we must understand what a human actually is. We are not merely bodies with brains. According to Scripture, humans are made up of three distinct yet integrated parts: spirit, soul, and body.

Genesis 2:7 tells us, "Then the Lord God formed the man of dust from the ground and breathed into his nostrils the breath of life, and the man became a living soul."

This verse reveals something profound. The body came from the dust of the earth. The spirit came from the breath of God. And the union of the two produced a living soul, your mind, will, and emotions. You are not just your skin. You are not just your personality. You are not even just your consciousness. You are a spiritual being living in a body, guided by a soul.

To make it simple, your body is your earth suit. It connects you to the physical world through senses, touch, sight, taste, smell, and hearing. Your soul is your inner person. It's where you think, feel, remember, and choose. It holds your identity and personality. Your spirit is your eternal part. It's the part of you that communes with God, receives revelation, and connects to the unseen world.

Each part is important, but not equal in authority. In God's design, your spirit should lead, your soul should agree, and your body should follow. But when sin enters or trauma disrupts, this order is flipped, the body demands, the soul panics, and the spirit goes silent.

That's where the enemy attacks. He whispers to your soul through emotional wounds, hoping you will follow feelings rather than faith.

When a person chooses suicide, they end the function of the body, but not the soul or spirit. The body may die, but the soul, your emotions, memories, regrets, and awareness, continues.

The spirit, which should be connected to God, may now find itself completely severed from the Source of life, especially if the person never surrendered to Christ.

Jesus warned in Matthew 10:28, "Do not fear those who kill the body but cannot kill the soul. Rather fear him who can destroy both soul and body in hell."

Hell is not just physical destruction, it is spiritual torment. And that torment begins not when you're judged by God, but the moment your soul leaves your body without His covering.

The Spirit Behind Suicide

One of the most terrifying truths about spiritual death is this: you are still fully conscious. You remember everything. You feel everything. You know you exist. And if you enter eternity apart from God, you cannot escape that awareness.

Suicide is often driven by the desire to stop the pain. But what happens if the pain doesn't stop, if it intensifies? What if the sadness, confusion, and darkness follow you because they were never just emotions, but entities that had been given access to your soul?

This is the hidden truth the spirit of suicide doesn't want you to know. It convinces people they are ending the suffering, when in reality, they may be sealing it.

You were not created for death. You were created to live, physically, emotionally, and spiritually. That's why suicide feels so unnatural. It breaks God's original design.

Even in your most broken moment, your soul knows something is wrong. That's why guilt, fear, and hesitation often rush in before the act. These are not signs of weakness, they are alerts from your spirit screaming, "Don't do this. There is still life!"

And God is not silent in these moments. He speaks through conviction, through memories of love, through the presence of a friend, or even through these words on this page. He is always calling you back.

Tampering with Spiritual Boundaries

God sets spiritual boundaries for our protection. Life and death are not to be handled casually. Instead, the Word tells us to seek relationship with Christ, who gives us the Holy Spirit to guide us safely.

Suicide is a forced entry into the spiritual world without God's direction. It's the ultimate violation of spiritual boundaries, not exploration but abandonment.

And the spirit of suicide? It whispers that the other side is peaceful, calm, or even beautiful. But it never tells you who is waiting for you on the other side.

Every death, natural or unnatural, is followed by a spiritual encounter. Scripture is clear: "It is appointed unto man once to die, and after this the judgment" (Hebrews 9:27). The moment your soul leaves your body, it does not wander aimlessly, it is met.

In Luke 16:22. 23, Jesus shares a story of two men: a poor man named Lazarus and a rich man. Lazarus died and was carried by angels to Abraham's side (a picture of peace and paradise). The rich man died and found himself in torment, fully conscious, begging for relief.

Notice what Jesus did not say: that death was the end. Both men remained fully aware of their surroundings, choices, and condition. This same pattern is true for everyone. Upon death, you are greeted either by the presence of God and His angels, if you belonged to Him, or by dark spiritual beings if you lived apart from Christ.

The spirit of suicide is a liar. It tells you death is an escape, but it never tells you that you might be jumping into eternal bondage.

The Spirit Behind Suicide

Your life reflects your allegiance, whether to God or to darkness. If you have surrendered to Christ, even in your struggle, He covers you with grace. But if your heart has rejected Him or if you die unrepentant, especially by taking your own life, you may find yourself outside of His covering, greeted not by peace, but by torment.

Demons don't just want your moment of pain, they want your eternity. They don't mind comforting you with lies if it helps them harvest your soul.

This is why the decision to live is not just about earthly peace, it's about eternal destiny.

For those who have struggled, who have loved God but fell into despair, we do not pronounce condemnation. But we must sound the alarm: suicide is not safe. It is not neutral.

Jesus died to give us life, not death. He took the torment so we wouldn't have to. Choosing to follow Him, even in the midst of pain, is the only safe passage from this world to the next.

Reflection Questions

Use these questions for personal reflection, journaling, or in conversation with a trusted mentor or counselor. Be honest, be vulnerable, and invite God into your processing.

1. Have you ever heard thoughts that sounded like whispers suggesting suicide? Can you now recognize those voices as spiritual, not just emotional?

2. What pain or trauma in your life feels overwhelming right now? Bring it before God in prayer. He wants your honesty more than your perfection.

3. Do you truly understand the eternal consequences of suicide, not just for your body, but for your soul? What part of this truth challenges or sobers you the most?

4. How can you strengthen your spirit so that it leads, rather than letting your emotions and body rule you? Are you feeding your spirit daily with prayer, Scripture, and worship?

Key Takeaways

- Suicide is not just a mental or emotional struggle, it is a spiritual battle influenced by demonic deception.

- The spirit of suicide whispers lies like "You'll find peace," "No one cares," and "This is your only option." These thoughts are not from God.

- At the moment of death, your soul does not end, it transitions into the spiritual realm and remains fully conscious.

- You are a three-part being: spirit, soul, and body. Suicide destroys the body but launches the soul into eternity, potentially without God.

- Upon death, you are greeted either by angels or demons, depending on who you served in life.

- God's mercy is deep, but suicide is not a doorway to peace, it is often a trap into deeper torment.

- You are loved by God, created with purpose, and called to live. Hope is real, healing is possible, and eternity is worth waiting for.

PART II

THE DEMONIC ARCHITECTURE OF DESPAIR

CHAPTER 4

THE LIE OF WORTHLESSNESS

"Even the very hairs of your head are all numbered. Fear not therefore; you are of more value than many sparrows.". Luke 12:7

There is a voice that speaks not with sound but with shame, a voice that whispers, you are nothing, you are forgotten, you are beyond repair. It is not the voice of your Maker, but of the accuser who delights in distorting the image of God within man. The lie of worthlessness is one of the most venomous weapons of the enemy because it does not strike from outside; it festers within. It is not a visible wound but an inward corrosion that eats at one's confidence, holiness, and sense of divine belonging.

When man believes he is worthless, he becomes an empty altar. The fire of devotion cannot burn on a heart that sees no reason to offer itself. The lie of worthlessness silences worship, weakens prayer, and defiles identity. It makes man bow not before the throne of grace, but before the mirror of failure.

The adversary knows that as long as a believer doubts his worth, he cannot walk in dominion. This is why the first warfare of the mind is not against lust, fear, or pride, it is against the lie that says, you are not enough for God to use. Yet Scripture reveals a different testimony: "You are a chosen generation, a royal priesthood, a holy nation, a peculiar people" (1 Peter 2:9). These are not titles for the perfect but for the redeemed.

Every time the enemy whispers unworthiness, he attempts to erase the cross. For the cross is God's eternal statement that humanity is worth redeeming. The blood of Jesus is not a cheap commodity, it is the currency of heaven's valuation. You cannot be worthless when God paid Himself for you.

The Weight of Shame and the Silence of Worship

To believe the lie of worthlessness is to believe that the blood was wasted. To accept the voice of shame is to reject the voice that cried, "It is finished." Many walk under the weight of past sins, feeling unfit for the altar of holiness. But the altar was built for the broken, not for the flawless. The fire of God falls where repentance burns, not where perfection stands.

There are those who fast, pray, and labor in ministry, yet deep within, they are haunted by the echo of insignificance. They preach deliverance but feel bound by self-condemnation. They declare faith yet doubt their own acceptance. This contradiction births exhaustion. It is not sin that kills them, but shame. The lie of worthlessness turns servants of light into slaves of guilt.

It is written, "There is therefore now no condemnation to them which are in Christ Jesus" (Romans 8:1). Condemnation is the counterfeit of conviction. The Holy Spirit convicts to restore, but the enemy condemns to destroy. When you hear a voice that leads you away from the throne of grace, that voice is not holy, it is hellish.

The tragedy of this generation is that we have equated self-esteem with worth. But worth is not built by human affirmation; it is defined by divine creation. You are not valuable because people see your light, you are valuable because God spoke you into being. He does not manufacture accidents; He births purpose. Before you failed, He already forgave. Before you stumbled, He already ordained your restoration.

You must learn to separate guilt from identity. Guilt says, "I did wrong." Shame says, "I am wrong." One is an act; the other is a verdict. The blood of Jesus erases the verdict and purifies the act. When He said, "You are clean through the word I have spoken," He was not describing temporary purity but positional holiness.

BREAKING SUICIDAL THOUGHTS

The lie of worthlessness thrives in silence. It grows where confession dies. When you hide your pain, you empower your prison. Healing begins when you bring your wounds to the altar of light. Confession is not weakness; it is warfare. Every time you bring your hidden sin into the light, you destroy the power of darkness that feeds on secrecy.

Do not call yourself unworthy when the Lamb has called you beloved. Do not wear shame as your identity when Jesus wore the crown of thorns in your place. The thorns that pierced His head were the thoughts that torment yours. He took your mental agony upon His own brow so that your mind might rest in His peace.

There is no such thing as a worthless vessel, only one that has forgotten its Potter. The hands that molded the heavens are the same hands that shaped your soul. You are not a mistake in process; you are a masterpiece in formation. God does not discard clay because it cracked; He remolds it. The altar of restoration is for the marred, not the magnificent.

If you listen long enough to the lie of worthlessness, you will begin to interpret divine silence as divine rejection. But silence is not absence, it is strategy. God hides not because He is distant but because He is drawing you deeper. Every silence is a summons to seek. Every delay is an invitation to trust.

When Elijah hid in the cave, the voice of the Lord did not thunder through the earthquake or blaze through the fire, it came as a whisper. Because sometimes, to hear the truth of your worth, you must quiet the noise of your pain.

The voice of worthlessness will always speak louder than truth until you choose which one to feed. You cannot meditate on your failures and expect faith to grow. The altar you feed determines the fire you carry. If you feed shame, you birth silence. If you feed truth, you birth confidence.

The Goal of the Enemy

The enemy's ultimate goal is not to make you sin but to make you quit. Once he convinces you that you are beyond redemption, he no longer has to tempt you, you will self-destruct. The most dangerous warfare is not fought in the flesh but in the thoughts.

Paul understood this when he wrote, "Casting down imaginations, and every high thing that exalteth itself against the knowledge of God." The knowledge of God is your shield against inferiority. Every thought that questions God's love for you is an altar of deceit. Tear it down.

The Lord never called anyone worthless, yet the devil never called anyone valuable. The two voices cannot coexist in your spirit. You must decide which sound will govern your identity, the voice of truth or the whisper of shame.

The greatest deception of the lie of worthlessness is that it disguises itself as humility. Many believers mistake self-hatred for holiness. But there is no holiness in despising what God has redeemed. True humility is agreement with God's truth, not denial of His work. When you call yourself worthless, you argue with the cross. When you say, "I am nothing," yet God says, "You are Mine," who then is the liar?

Humility does not mean thinking less of yourself; it means thinking of yourself through God's eyes. It is recognizing that every good in you is His reflection, not your merit. The devil has convinced many that the only way to be holy is to feel small. But holiness is not humiliation, it is alignment. It is living in the identity purchased by the blood.

Even the prophets wrestled with worth. Isaiah cried, "Woe is me, for I am undone," yet in that moment, the seraph flew with a live coal from the altar and touched his lips, saying, "Your iniquity is taken away." The moment Isaiah confessed his unworthiness, heaven did not agree, it purified him. The throne never echoes condemnation; it releases cleansing.

If you have failed, rise again. The fall was not meant to define you but to refine you. God uses broken men to build unbreakable altars. Your scars are not shame, they are signatures of grace. The same Peter who denied Jesus three times became the apostle of power on the day of Pentecost. Grace rewrites history without erasing truth.

The lie of worthlessness kills destiny before it begins. When Moses said, "I am not eloquent," he thought his weakness disqualified him. But God said, "Who made man's mouth?" When Jeremiah said, "I am a child," God replied, "Say not, I am a child." Heaven does not entertain inferiority; it commands obedience. You are not the author of your calling. He is. And He never calls whom He will not enable.

Every time you bow to the lie of worthlessness, you mock divine election. God does not choose the qualified; He qualifies the chosen. The proof of His power is not in your perfection but in your dependence. When you feel unworthy, do not retreat,. kneel. When you feel inadequate, do not hide, surrender. The altar of worth is found in yieldedness.

The Lie of Worthlessness

The kingdom operates by divine exchange: He gives beauty for ashes, joy for mourning, praise for heaviness. The reason worthlessness is a lie is because Jesus already bore it. He became despised so that you might be accepted. He became rejected so that you might be embraced. The worth of a thing is measured by the price paid for it. You are worth the blood of the Lamb.

Let every chain of inferiority break where this truth enters. Let every altar of shame be consumed by the fire of revelation. Let every mind that has believed the lie of worthlessness be renewed by the voice of the Word. You are not defined by what you have done, but by who has redeemed you. You are not measured by your past, but by your covenant. You are not shaped by men's rejection, but by divine affection.

Lift your head. You are a vessel of light. You are a temple of the Spirit. You are the habitation of holiness. The same Spirit that raised Christ from the dead lives in you. The same power that spoke the galaxies now calls you son. The throne does not tolerate worthlessness; it transforms it into worship.

When you look into the mirror, do not see what sin made of you, see what grace is making of you. The Potter is not done. The cracks are not final. The fire is not for your destruction but for your distinction. Every furnace is a refiner's altar, and when you emerge, the gold of identity will shine.

Let the weak say, "I am strong." Let the broken say, "I am healed." Let the ashamed say, "I am redeemed." For worthlessness cannot dwell where revelation lives. The light of His truth is the death of every lie.

Reflection Questions

1. In what ways have you unknowingly agreed with the lie of worthlessness in your thoughts or speech?

2. How does understanding that worth is defined by the blood change your view of yourself?

3. What are the altars in your life where shame still speaks louder than grace?

4. Have you confused humility with self-hatred? How can you realign your definition of humility to reflect truth instead of shame?

5. What does it mean for you personally that the Potter is not done?

Key Takeaways

- Worthlessness is a satanic distortion of divine identity. God never calls His redeemed worthless.
- Humility is agreement with truth, not denial of grace.
- The altar of shame must be replaced with the altar of light.
- The measure of your worth is the blood that bought you.

- Every silence of God is not rejection but invitation to deeper trust.
- The Potter does not discard clay. He remolds it.

CHAPTER 5

THE HIDDEN BATTLE IN THE MIND

"For though we walk in the flesh, we do not war after the flesh.". 2 Corinthians 10:3

BREAKING SUICIDAL THOUGHTS

Suicidal ideation rarely begins as a violent shout. More often, it starts as a faint whisper: No one would miss you. You're a burden. It will never get better. These thoughts do not arrive like external intrusions; they disguise themselves as inner conclusions, logical reflections on pain. And because they sound like your own reasoning, you may not discern how foreign, dark, and strategic they truly are.

Your mind is like a garden, and every thought is a seed. Some seeds sprout quickly and vanish, but others take root, especially when watered by repetition or emotion. Over time, a thought like I'm a failure can mature into a mental stronghold, a deeply embedded belief that shapes how you see yourself, your world, and your future.

That is why Scripture declares, "As a man thinks in his heart, so is he" (Proverbs 23:7). The condition of your mind determines the direction of your life. When suicidal thoughts are entertained, even briefly, they begin to distort perception. A breakup is no longer a heartbreak; it becomes proof that you are unlovable. A job loss is no longer a setback; it becomes evidence that you are worthless. This is the hidden warfare of the adversary: he does not strike the body first, but the mind.

Satan seldom introduces himself when he whispers lies. He is a master of camouflage, planting his voice inside familiar thought patterns. In the Garden of Eden, he did not roar as a lion; he slithered in as a subtle serpent. His words to Eve were quiet, logical, and laced with doubt: "Did God really say…?" That is still how he speaks.

To the weary, he murmurs: Wouldn't it be easier to just sleep forever?

To the ashamed: You'll never change. Why keep trying? To the grieving: If you were gone, maybe the pain would stop.

These whispers do not sound demonic, they sound human. They echo your tone, your memory, your voice. That is the trap. He plants a lie and waits for you to water it. Once you agree, the lie merges with your identity and becomes a belief system.

Life and Death in the Mind

Every suicidal act begins with a thought. That is why the Bible says, "The mind governed by the flesh is death, but the mind governed by the Spirit is life and peace" (Romans 8:6). When your mind is ruled by wounds, fear, or demonic influence, it spirals toward despair. But when your mind is filled with the Spirit, it begins to birth hope, strength, and clarity.

God gave you a sacred weapon: your will. The enemy may suggest thoughts, but he cannot control them unless you permit him. You have authority, in Christ, to reject lies and replace them with truth. But first, you must recognize the pattern.

Understanding how suicidal thoughts take root helps you trace their origin and uproot them. The lie of death feeds on seeds of pain, each germinating under different soil conditions of the heart.

When rejection and abandonment pierce your soul, the lie arrives: You are unwanted. That seed grows quickly when watered with isolation.

BREAKING SUICIDAL THOUGHTS

When shame and guilt follow failure, the enemy tries to convert an event into identity, whispering, You are your mistake. You'll never recover.

When trauma, through abuse, betrayal, or violence, remains unhealed, it becomes an open gate through which the spirit of suicide whispers escape.

When demonic influence disguises itself as comfort, it pretends to offer peace while preparing destruction. The spirit of suicide does not shout, it soothes, until death feels like rest.

And finally, when hopelessness sets in, the soul reaches its lowest ebb. At that stage, a person may not want to die, they simply cannot imagine living. Death begins to masquerade as relief.

Yet to have a suicidal thought does not mean you are evil, faithless, or lost. It means you are under attack. And attacks can be resisted.

The human brain is wired for patterns. It thrives on repetition and reinforcement. That is how habits are formed, not only physical ones but mental ones too. When a thought is repeated often enough, your brain builds a neurological pathway for it, much like a trail worn down by frequent steps. Soon, that thought becomes automatic, replaying subconsciously. This is what Scripture calls a stronghold; science calls it a loop.

Thought loops are not inherently negative. Repeating Scripture, gratitude, or truth creates godly patterns that renew the mind and restore peace. But when loops are built from pain, shame, or oppression, they become toxic and self-destructive. Among the most deadly are suicidal thought loops.

Imagine a mind rehearsing this silent mantra: I always mess things up. No one cares about me. I'll never be free from this pain. Maybe the world would be better off without me. Each sentence becomes a brick. Over time, these bricks form a fortress, a stronghold of despair.

Strongholds are not physical, they are psychological and spiritual prisons where lies are defended as truth. Even when someone speaks hope, the stronghold filters it out: They don't really know me. If they did, they'd agree with my pain.

Paul understood this when he wrote, "The weapons of our warfare are not carnal but mighty through God for pulling down strongholds, casting down imaginations, and every high thing that exalts itself against the knowledge of God" (2 Corinthians 10:4. 5).

Notice the battlefront, arguments, imaginations, and high things. These are not demons in the air but belief systems in the mind. Prideful conclusions, false perceptions, and self-condemnations that exalt themselves against divine truth.

To dismantle suicidal thought loops, you must walk in four sacred steps.

First, identify the lie. Name the words that have been echoing in your mind. Bring them from the darkness into the light. You cannot confront what you refuse to name.

Second, expose the source. Ask: Is this thought from God, from truth, from the Word? Or is it birthed from trauma, fear, or accusation? Every thought has a father, either the Father of Light or the father of lies.

Third, replace it with truth. Do not simply evict the lie; enthrone the truth. For every lie, there is a divine counter-statement.

When the lie says, No one loves me, the truth answers: "I have loved you with an everlasting love" (Jeremiah 31:3).

When the lie says, There's no way out, the truth declares: "God is faithful…He will also provide a way out so that you can endure it" (1 Corinthians 10:13).

Finally, repeat the truth until it becomes louder. Just as repetition fortified the lie, repetition will now reinforce truth. You are not engaging in self-hypnosis, you are restoring divine order to your mental realm.

Not every thought pattern is psychological; some are spiritual. Certain loops are sustained by demonic attachment. Evil spirits exploit trauma and rejection, rehearsing old pain to keep you bound. They do not merely whisper, they echo. They replay scenes, amplify guilt, and exhaust the will until surrender feels easier than resistance.

This is why spiritual warfare is essential. Therapy is good. Counseling is wise. Medication may stabilize, but deliverance renews. The root must be addressed in the realm of the Spirit. Jesus said, "You shall know the truth, and the truth shall make you free" (John 8:32). That truth is not theory, it is power.

When Jesus was tempted in the wilderness, Satan used Scripture out of context to manipulate His mind. But Jesus did not argue emotionally. He countered with truth. He said, "It is written…" (Matthew 4). He modeled the perfect pattern for mental warfare.

Every time the enemy whispers death, declare life. When he says, You'll never be free, respond, It is written: He whom the Son sets free is free indeed. When he says, End it all, declare, It is written: I shall not die, but live, and declare the works of the Lord (Psalm 118:17).

Truth is not information, it is a sword. Ephesians 6:17 calls it "the sword of the Spirit." When spoken in faith, truth cuts through deception, pierces through fog, and silences accusation.

You are not helpless. You are not insane. You are armed with the mind of Christ (1 Corinthians 2:16), a mind of clarity, purity, and dominion.

When the mind begins to shift under the weight of God's truth, an atmosphere change takes place. What once felt like darkness and confusion becomes a field of divine light. The mind is not simply a place of thoughts; it is a gate, either opening toward the Spirit of life or the spirit of death. Every gate must have a keeper. When the gate of the mind is left unguarded, unfiltered voices enter freely, planting seeds of distortion. But when the mind is guarded by truth, worship, and the fear of the Lord, it becomes a sanctuary, a resting place for the thoughts of Christ.

This is why the Word says, "You will keep him in perfect peace, whose mind is stayed on You." (Isaiah 26:3). Perfect peace is not the absence of struggle, it is the authority of divine order within your thought realm. It is when heaven's truth governs your inner conversation. To keep your mind stayed on God means to continually align every emotion, memory, and conclusion to His nature.

Peace is not passive, it is a warfare stance. The believer who wins the battle of the mind wins the war of destiny.

Renewing the mind is not a one-time event but a continual act of surrender. Every day, thoughts rise like waves, demanding your agreement. Each thought seeks to sit upon the throne of your attention. The one you enthrone becomes the one you serve.

Paul's exhortation in Romans 12:2 is not psychological, it is priestly: "Be transformed by the renewing of your mind." Transformation is worship. It happens as we lay every corrupted pattern on the altar of truth and receive new patterns from the Spirit. In this process, the altar is not physical, it is within your consciousness. You bring your memories, your pain, your imaginations, and lay them down before God, saying, "Lord, burn away every falsehood and renew my mind with Your Word."

Each time you surrender a lie, a portion of your spiritual sight is restored. Each time you choose truth, a gate of revelation opens. The mind becomes illuminated, and your spirit begins to perceive reality as heaven sees it.

Breaking the Covenant with Death

Isaiah 28:18 declares, "Your covenant with death shall be disannulled, and your agreement with hell shall not stand." Suicidal thoughts are not just mental, they are covenantal. The enemy seeks to forge an invisible pact through agreement. Every time you silently agree with the voice that says, "It would be better if I were gone," you unknowingly sign an invisible contract in the spirit. But when you renounce that agreement, by the Word of God and the authority of Jesus' blood, the covenant is broken.

Declare aloud: "I break every agreement with death. I reject the lies of despair. I come into covenant with life, truth, and hope in Jesus Christ."

This declaration is more than words, it is warfare. The blood of Jesus enforces it. The moment you say it in faith, the Spirit of Life begins to uproot every death-seed in your mind.

Every thought is an altar where worship is offered, either to God or to darkness. When your mind dwells on hope, you raise an altar of light. When your thoughts feed on despair, you raise an altar of death. This is why worship and meditation are not just emotional acts, they are altar acts. They determine who reigns over your mental realm.

The Lord desires to reclaim the territory of your thoughts, to establish His government within your imagination. He wants your mind to mirror His throne, full of order, light, and holiness.

To reclaim your mental altar, you must consistently do three things:

1. Renounce every lie that defiles the mind's purity.
2. Consecrate your thought life as worship unto God.
3. Feed continually on the Word until your default atmosphere becomes light.

Over time, your mental climate changes. The air of your thoughts becomes holy ground. The enemy loses entry.

Every serpent thrives in darkness. Suicidal thoughts multiply in secrecy. But when light enters, through confession, through

Scripture, through prayer, the serpent is exposed and loses its grip. Ephesians 5:13 says, "Everything exposed by the light becomes visible, and everything that is illuminated becomes a light."

When you bring your hidden pain into God's light, He transforms even your wounds into weapons. The very places where despair tried to destroy you become testimonies of divine power. You become a light to others walking through shadowed valleys.

If the enemy builds strongholds of lies, then God builds fortresses of truth. Proverbs 18:10 declares, "The name of the Lord is a strong tower; the righteous run into it and are safe." The process of mental healing is not just tearing down, it is rebuilding.

Here's how you rebuild the fortress of your mind:

- Lay a foundation of Scripture. Choose daily verses and meditate until they become instinctive responses to pain.
- Guard your gates. What you watch, hear, and imagine either reinforces truth or resurrects deception.
- Anchor your emotions in worship. Don't let your feelings dictate truth; let truth sanctify your feelings.
- Live in confession and accountability. Transparency keeps the mind clean. Hiddenness breeds infestation.

The goal is not to have a mind empty of thoughts, but a mind filled with holy order.

Hope is heaven's language in the midst of human despair. It is not optimism; it is revelation. Hope declares that what God said is truer than what I feel. Romans 15:13 says, "May the God of hope fill you with all joy and peace in believing." Notice, it is not the absence of struggle that fills you with peace; it is believing.

Every time you choose to believe God's promise over your pain, you enter covenant with hope. Hope then becomes an anchor, keeping your soul steady when storms rage. It whispers, "You will live and not die. You will see the goodness of God in the land of the living."

The spirit of suicide cannot dwell in a soul anchored in hope. It needs hopelessness to breathe. Starve it by feeding your faith.

Reflection Questions

1. Which thoughts in your life have felt like permanent residents rather than visitors? Are they life-giving or life-draining?

2. What "agreements" with despair have you unknowingly made through repeated internal dialogue?

3. How can you begin turning your thought life into an altar of worship this week?

4. Who can walk with you in prayer and accountability to ensure your mental gates remain guarded?

Key Takeaways

- Thoughts become strongholds; strongholds become agreements; agreements become covenants. Break every covenant with death and replace it with covenantal truth.
- Hope is not emotional, it is divine revelation that anchors you through every storm.
- You are not alone in this battle. Heaven fights with you. The Spirit of Life dwells in you.
- Your renewed mind will not only preserve your life, it will deliver others trapped in despair.

CHAPTER 6

THE STAGES OF SPIRITUAL INFILTRATION

"Be sober, be vigilant; because your adversary the devil walks about like a roaring lion, seeking whom he may devour.". 1 Peter 5:8

BREAKING SUICIDAL THOUGHTS

It often begins in silence, not a loud crash, not an open confrontation, but a whisper that feels like your own thought. It enters softly, like a suggestion wrapped in weariness. "You're tired." "No one really cares." "It would be easier if you weren't here." These words sound harmless at first, just echoes of exhaustion, reflections of pain, but they are not yours. They come from a realm that studies your patterns, watches your pain, and waits for permission to enter.

Spiritual oppression is the earliest stage of demonic influence. It operates through suggestion, heaviness, and pressure. The enemy doesn't need to roar when a whisper will do. He slips thoughts through the cracks of discouragement, feeding them to the mind until you mistake them for truth. It is here that most battles of suicide begin, not with an action, but with an idea.

The whisper of darkness gains strength through repetition. Every time you entertain it, it gains ground. Every time you replay the thought, it grows roots in the soil of your imagination. The oppression isn't just emotional; it's atmospheric. You feel the heaviness in your room. The silence becomes thick, almost breathing. Hope feels distant, and though you can't see anything, something unseen feels near, watching, waiting, whispering.

Oppression is like an entity that walks beside you, mimicking your voice, rehearsing your pain. It feeds on isolation. When you pull away from people, it tightens its grip. When you stop praying, it grows louder. When you turn off the light, it sits at the edge of your bed, whispering doubts into the corners of your mind. Its goal is not immediate destruction but slow surrender, to make you too weary to resist.

Every dark spirit thrives on deception, and its greatest lie is normalcy. It wants you to think this is simply "how life feels." It wants you to normalize heaviness, to call despair by natural names. "I'm just tired," "I'm just stressed," "It's just life." But no, this heaviness carries personality. It is intelligent, patient, and strategic. It studies your pain, searching for doors left open through trauma, shame, or neglect.

When oppression deepens, it begins to test your emotional temperature. It studies how you react to rejection, to fear, to loneliness. If a particular wound makes you crumble, it presses there repeatedly. It waits for you to agree with its language, for you to echo its lies: "I'm worthless." "I'll never change." "Maybe everyone would be better without me." Every agreement becomes a contract, however small. Every repeated lie becomes an opening for the next stage.

Once the darkness realizes you are listening, it becomes bolder. The whispers no longer come as questions; they come as conclusions. "You are hopeless." "You cannot be loved." "There is no future." By this point, oppression is maturing into obsession, the next phase of infiltration.

The Soul's Compromise

When obsession begins, the spirit no longer whispers from the outside. It starts to echo from within. It begins to sound like you. You no longer hear "a voice", you feel a conviction. The thought pattern embeds itself so deeply that you cannot separate your identity from your despair. You begin to believe, "This is who I am."

This is where darkness tightens its grip. The line between your pain and its presence begins to blur. You wake up already tired.

BREAKING SUICIDAL THOUGHTS

You sleep but do not rest. You smile publicly but feel hollow privately. You pray but hear nothing. You start thinking about the end, not because you want to die, but because you want relief.

In obsession, the spiritual invasion shifts from occasional to constant. The demonic voice no longer knocks; it lives in the house. You feel trapped inside your own mind, the same thought looping endlessly. It plays like background music: "You're not enough." "There's no escape." "You can't fix this." It's not random; it's a campaign. The goal is to wear you down until you surrender.

At this stage, many people begin to experience strange mental or emotional fluctuations, sudden hopelessness, violent thoughts, irrational guilt, or even physical heaviness. These are not just psychological waves; they are spiritual attempts to weaken resistance. The enemy's goal is simple: to make you agree. Because the moment you agree. "Yes, maybe I am worthless," "Yes, maybe I'd be better gone", you authorize the next level of control.

This is the soul's compromise, when a person begins to accept darkness as truth. Every human being is a house with windows and doors, thoughts are the windows, emotions are the doors. The enemy cannot enter unless invited. But despair, when embraced, becomes that invitation. The whispering spirit finds a place to anchor itself in your emotions, and that foothold becomes obsession.

And yet, even here, there is still room for light. The Spirit of God never forces entry but always offers rescue. Sometimes, that rescue comes as a phone call, a song, a sudden memory, or even this book you are reading. These interruptions are not coincidences; they are lifelines, divine breaches in the enemy's design. The darkness fears interruption because it thrives in secrecy. Exposure breaks its spell.

So if you ever find yourself wrestling with the same hopeless thoughts repeatedly, know this: you are not losing your mind, you are under attack. And the attack can be resisted. The voice is not stronger than your will, and your will can still turn toward light. The mere act of recognizing that these thoughts are not you is already an act of defiance. Awareness is resistance. Naming the darkness dethrones it.

Possession

By the time a spirit reaches the stage of possession, the inner war has shifted from influence to control. The voice that once whispered suggestions now commands. The darkness that once waited at the door now sits in the driver's seat of the mind. The person becomes a prisoner inside his or her own emotions, still conscious, still thinking, yet overridden by a power that manipulates impulse and overrides resistance.

Possession doesn't always look like the dramatic scenes people imagine. It can wear normal clothes, smile on the outside, and function at work. The difference is internal: the person no longer has full say over their thoughts, moods, or actions. The oppression has matured into ownership. The enemy has moved from influence to residence.

This possession stage is rare for those who still retain awareness of God's voice or truth, but it happens to those who, through long rejection of light, lose distinction between themselves and the invading darkness. They no longer resist. Their emotional walls collapse; their conscience becomes numb. What was once a whisper now sounds like destiny: "It's time to end it. It's the only way." The mind no longer debates, it obeys.

Possession isn't simply spiritual; it's also neurological. The demonic presence hijacks the natural chemistry of the brain, amplifying despair, accelerating impulse, and dulling reason. The person feels compelled, like an invisible hand is pushing them forward. In their final moments, a deceptive calm often sets in. The storm in their thoughts quiets. It feels like peace, but it's the silence before captivity.

In the unseen realm, the spirits that engineered this deception celebrate. They have succeeded in their oldest ambition: to destroy what God created in His image. The human body that once carried light becomes a battlefield trophy. The soul, confused and disoriented, awakens beyond the body, realizing too late that the calm was a trap.

Demons do not appear with horns or fire; they manifest through thought, energy, and fear. Their laughter is not heard with the ear but felt in the soul, a vibration of mockery that echoes, "We won another." They rejoice not in the person's pain but in their separation from purpose. Every suicide is a statement of rebellion against the Creator, and in that act, darkness feels vindicated.

Possession finalizes what oppression began: the breaking of the human will. The greatest tragedy is that, all along, the person's authority remained intact. The enemy never truly had power, only persuasion. But deception makes persuasion feel like command. The moment a person believes the lie. "I have no choice", the enemy wins.

The possessed mind becomes a stage for two audiences: heaven weeping, and hell applauding. The angels who once stood ready to protect watch as human choice locks the door from the inside. They cannot override free will. The Holy Spirit withdraws not in anger, but in sorrow, because love never forces itself. The light grows dim, not because it was defeated, but because it was rejected.

And yet, even as the spirit departs from the body, heaven does not gloat. The mercy of God mourns. The soul, stepping beyond the physical realm, realizes that the voices it trusted were lies. The peace it expected becomes confusion. There is awareness, instant and unbearable, that the deception was complete. The darkness it embraced now surrounds it. What once felt like a friend becomes a captor.

The Eternal Realization

In that instant, the human soul understands too late that suicide was not an escape from pain, but an entrance into greater torment, not inflicted by God, but by the company it kept. Demonic entities, having lured the person through despair, now rejoice in ownership. The laughter that follows is not celebration but cruelty, a perverse triumph that mocks both the victim and the Creator.

For those who lived without knowledge of divine truth, the transition into the spirit world is jarring. The environment matches their inner state, cold, echoing, and void of light. There is no sound but regret. The once-familiar voices now taunt. "You believed us," they whisper. "You thought death would help." The soul realizes that the pain didn't end; it merely changed dimension.

But for those who had once known grace, the experience is even more piercing. Memory remains. Awareness remains. The soul remembers every chance ignored, every whisper of hope dismissed. The voice of God, though distant, still echoes, not condemning, but grieving: "Why didn't you call My name?"

This realization is the deepest sorrow: to know that freedom was always possible, that light had never left, that help had always been waiting. The demons knew this truth, which is why they fought so hard to silence it. They wanted the person to believe that God was silent, absent, or indifferent. But the silence was never absence, it was patience.

Possession ends not with victory for darkness, but with tragedy for creation. Hell never creates; it only corrupts. The possessed are not trophies of conquest but casualties of deception. And though their choice is final, their story becomes a warning to the living: resist early, resist often, resist completely.

Reflection Questions

1. Can you recall moments when despair began to sound like your own voice?
2. How do you distinguish between your true thoughts and those that seek to harm you?
3. Why is recognizing spiritual deception early so crucial?
4. How does understanding these stages change the way you see mental battles?

Key Takeaways

- Darkness does not invade suddenly; it progresses through stages of consent.
- Oppression begins with whispers, obsession continues with internal agreement, possession ends with control.
- The mind is a sacred territory, once surrendered, it becomes a battlefield.
- Awareness and resistance are the first victories over spiritual infiltration.

CHAPTER 7

WHAT HAPPENS AT THE MOMENT OF DEATH

"It is appointed unto men once to die, but after this the judgment.". Hebrews 9:27

BREAKING SUICIDAL THOUGHTS

Before proceeding, I want to emphasize that this chapter expands upon certain mysteries already introduced in earlier chapters. While some themes may echo truths you have read before, this is intentional, because revelation deepens through repetition. Certain foundations must be reinforced for the fullness of understanding to emerge.

Death, from a purely biological lens, is defined as the irreversible cessation of vital function, when the heart stops, the lungs cease to breathe, and the brain becomes silent. But this definition touches only the shell of existence. For though the body expires, the spirit does not. The Word of God unveils what science cannot see, that man is spirit, soul, and body, and that death is not cessation, but separation.

As death nears, the body begins to yield its strength. The pulse weakens, breath becomes shallow, and the warmth of life slowly departs. Physicians call this the active dying phase, but Scripture calls it the loosening of the tent. When the final breath leaves the lungs and the blood ceases its flow, what the world calls the end is in truth a transition.

For at that moment, while men stand around a still form, there is motion in the unseen realm. The body lies silent, but the spirit stands awakened. Ecclesiastes 12:7 declares, "The dust returns to the earth as it was, and the spirit returns to God who gave it." The separation of spirit from body is not death's tragedy, it is its mystery.

To the natural eye, death is silence. But to the spirit, death is entrance. The veil between time and eternity tears, and the soul steps across into the realm it was created to inherit. Consciousness does not die, it intensifies.

The story of the rich man and Lazarus in Luke 16 remains one of Scripture's clearest unveilings. Both men died, yet both remained fully aware. One found comfort in the bosom of Abraham; the other found torment and thirst. This confirms that death does not end awareness, it transfers it.

When a man dies, he does not fade into oblivion. He crosses a threshold. And on that threshold, every hidden truth becomes visible, every deception exposed, every decision judged.

Many who contemplate suicide believe they are choosing rest. They imagine the darkness of death as relief from suffering. But death is not an escape from awareness, it is the doorway to intensified awareness in the spirit world. The soul that dies outside of Christ does not sleep; it awakens into judgment.

The tragedy of suicide is that it promises peace but delivers exposure. It claims to end pain but ushers the soul into a realm where pain is eternal if grace has been rejected. For once the soul steps beyond the veil, there is no undoing of choices.

You do not stop existing when you die. You simply change realms.

Understanding Spirit and Soul

Man is a triune creation: body, soul, and spirit. These three are distinct yet interwoven. The body is the visible vessel, formed from dust, fragile, and temporary. The soul houses your mind, emotions, and will, the essence of personality. The spirit is the eternal part of you that communes with God.

When death comes, the body returns to the ground, the soul departs, and the spirit stands before its Creator. The body without the spirit is lifeless, like a glove without a hand. The hand, the true essence, withdraws, and the glove becomes empty.

This is why our generation's obsession with the body is tragic. Culture magnifies what is perishing while neglecting what is eternal. The flesh may be adorned, but it cannot follow you beyond the grave. Paul calls the body a tent, fragile and fleeting, yet within it dwells an eternal inhabitant awaiting an immortal home (2 Corinthians 5:1).

When a man dies by suicide, the body ceases, but the spirit continues its journey, either toward light or darkness. Suicide cannot erase the self. It merely relocates it.

The soul lives between two pulls, the voice of the flesh and the call of the spirit. When despair rules the mind, and the emotions sink into darkness, the soul becomes vulnerable to deception. But when the spirit, renewed by the Holy Ghost, rises, it brings the soul under divine order.

The tragedy of suicide lies in this imbalance: the soul overtakes the spirit. The devil whispers to the mind, inflames emotion, and wears down the will. He plants lies that feel like logic. That is why Scripture commands: "Take every thought captive to the obedience of Christ." (2 Corinthians 10:5). A single ungoverned thought can become an altar of destruction.

Thoughts are not harmless, they are spiritual gates. Each agreement opens a realm. When the soul believes a lie, that lie becomes a spiritual covenant. When truth is believed, heaven establishes dominion. This is why protecting the mind is not optional; it is survival.

At the precise moment the body expires, the soul detaches and is immediately escorted into the spiritual realm. Jesus revealed this mystery through the story of Lazarus and the rich man. The poor man was carried by angels into paradise; the rich man found himself in torment.

Every death summons an escort, holy or unholy. Angels attend the redeemed, while dark entities await those who rejected grace. No one crosses the threshold of eternity alone.

For those who die in Christ, death is not a terror but a homecoming. Angels rejoice, and heaven receives them with honor. But for those who die in rebellion, especially through the doorway of suicide, the soul's transition is not into rest but into reckoning.

When the soul leaves the body, there is a moment of realization, an awakening sharper than any dream. Many near-death testimonies describe the feeling of floating above one's body or seeing the physical form from a distance. While experiences vary, the spiritual truth remains constant: separation is real.

The Bible confirms it beyond speculation. The body sleeps in the earth, but the soul does not sleep. Jesus told the thief, "Today you will be with Me in paradise," not someday after the resurrection. Consciousness continues, instantly and eternally.

To the righteous, that awareness is peace. To the unredeemed, it is torment. Death is not silence, it is revelation.

Unseen Escorts

Every soul is met. Heaven or hell never waits long. Angels are sent forth as ministering spirits to gather those who belong to the Lamb. But for those who lived under deception, demons await, the same spirits that tormented their minds in life now claim them in death.

This is the unseen war around every human life. Angels fight for your obedience; demons fight for your despair. Each voice seeks covenant, one unto life, the other unto destruction.

Those who die in Christ are escorted into light, peace, and unspeakable joy. Those who die under the spirit of suicide, having rejected truth, are seized by the same darkness that deceived them. The unseen realm is not neutral. It responds to spiritual ownership.

The Bible is clear that death does not end consciousness. The body may return to the earth, but the spirit remains aware. This is why Jesus' words to the thief on the cross are so powerful: "Today you will be with Me in paradise." The immediacy of that statement reveals that death is not a void; it is a transition.

When the soul departs the body, its awareness increases, not decreases. The blind will see. The deaf will hear. The hardened heart will suddenly understand everything it ignored in life. This is why death without Christ is the greatest tragedy, it brings perfect understanding too late.

The moment of separation is both mysterious and terrifying for those without the covering of the blood of Jesus. The unseen realm becomes visible, and what one served in life becomes one's companion in eternity.

Hebrews 9:27 declares that it is appointed for man to die once, and after that comes judgment. Judgment is not a process of discovery for God, it is a revelation for the soul. The decisions made in the realm of time are exposed in the realm of eternity. Nothing is hidden; nothing is lost.

For those who died in Christ, judgment becomes vindication, the confirmation of their redemption and righteousness through His sacrifice. For those who died without Him, judgment becomes exposure, the unveiling of rebellion and unrepented sin.

Every thought, word, and motive is weighed before the Throne of the Lamb. This is why suicide, though often born from unbearable pain, cannot be seen as an escape. It is a premature crossing into a courtroom where deception will no longer defend the soul.

When the body dies, the realms exchange authority. The natural realm releases its grip, and the spiritual realm asserts dominion. The soul, long influenced by both, is now fully claimed by one.

If a person lived submitted to the Spirit of God, the transition is one of peace. Angels surround, light envelops, and the soul is received into rest. But if one lived under the influence of rebellion, darkness, or deception, the transition is marked by confusion and dread.

In this realm, time ceases to exist. Regret becomes eternal, and longing has no remedy. The soul remembers, feels, and perceives more acutely than ever before. Every act of rebellion becomes a weight, and every rejected call of mercy becomes an echo in the corridors of eternity.

The Reality of Hell and Heaven

Jesus spoke more about hell than any other prophet or apostle, not to instill fear but to awaken urgency. Hell is not symbolic, it is the ultimate manifestation of separation from God. It is not merely darkness; it is the absence of Light. It is not merely torment; it is existence without the Presence.

Heaven, on the other hand, is not an abstract paradise. It is a realm of divine order, holiness, and eternal communion with the Creator. It is the dwelling place of the redeemed, those washed by the blood of the Lamb. Every tear is wiped away, every wound is healed, and every longing is satisfied in His glory.

This is why Jesus said, "I go to prepare a place for you." Heaven is not an accident, it is a prepared destination for prepared souls. Suicide may cut short the earthly journey, but it cannot bypass the divine order of judgment and accountability.

Once the soul crosses into eternity, there are no second chances. The eternal destiny of every human being is sealed by the choices made on earth. The time for repentance is before death, not after.

For those contemplating suicide, this truth must pierce the fog of despair: You are not choosing silence, you are choosing eternity. What follows that choice depends entirely on your relationship with Jesus Christ.

The blood that speaks mercy now will not plead after death. The voice that calls you gently today will thunder in judgment tomorrow. The same cross that offers life becomes the measure of accountability.

One of the most dangerous lies of the age is that death brings peace to the tormented. But the peace the world speaks of is not the shalom of God. It is the counterfeit silence of spiritual blindness.

Those who die outside Christ do not find peace, they encounter truth without mercy. The illusion of final rest evaporates in the presence of divine justice. For those who die in Christ, however, death truly is rest. It is completion, not escape; fulfillment, not finality.

The righteous do not cease to exist, they enter into joy. Their labor ends, but their life begins anew. The wicked, however, awaken to the harvest of their rebellion. This is why Jesus said, "Do not fear those who kill the body but cannot kill the soul; rather fear Him who can destroy both soul and body in hell."

What Happens at the Moment of Death

Every human being is eternal. The question is not whether one will exist forever, it is where one will exist forever. Death reveals the eternal identity of the soul.

The man or woman who has surrendered to the lordship of Jesus Christ will be transformed into the likeness of His glory. But the one who rejects Him remains in the state of rebellion that defined their earthly life. Eternity is not a reset; it is the continuation of alignment.

This is why the soul must be anchored now. Every thought, every habit, every desire is shaping your eternal posture. The altar you serve on earth determines the throne you stand before in heaven.

Even in the shadow of suicide, there remains one unshakable truth: Jesus saves. His mercy can reach the brink of despair. His grace can pull a soul back from the edge.

If you are reading this and wrestling with thoughts of death, know this, you are not beyond redemption. The very fact that breath remains in your lungs is proof that heaven has not closed your case.

There is still time to surrender. There is still a path back to light. The voice that once whispered hope still calls your name. Life is not over. Eternity waits, but it does not have to wait in darkness.

Before you say goodbye, know what truly lies beyond. Eternity is real. And your life still has a purpose.

Reflection Questions

These questions are designed to lead you deeper into personal reflection, prayer, and honest conversation with a trusted spiritual guide or counselor. Do not rush through them. Sit with them. Let the Holy Spirit reveal truth and bring clarity.

1. What beliefs do you currently hold about death? Are they rooted in Scripture, personal experiences, or cultural ideas? Are they bringing you peace or confusion?

2. How does understanding the separation of the soul from the body at death impact your thoughts on suicide? Does it make the spiritual consequences feel more real or sobering?

3. Have you ever sensed the nearness of the spiritual realm in moments of pain or crisis? What did that feel like? Looking back, can you see any signs of spiritual influence, good or evil, during those moments?

4. What is your current relationship with Jesus? If your life were to end today, where would your soul go based on that relationship? Be honest. God welcomes truth.

Key Takeaways

• Death is not the end, it is a doorway into eternity. While the body returns to dust, the soul remains fully conscious and enters the spiritual realm.

• There is no "soul sleep." At death, the soul is immediately ushered into one of two realities: life with God or separation from Him.

• Suicide severs the soul's connection to the body before its appointed time, making one vulnerable to the powers of darkness if not anchored in Christ.

• Angels escort those in Christ. But for those who die in rebellion or deception, demonic entities may claim the soul, resulting in torment rather than peace.

• The afterlife is not neutral. Your choices in this life shape your eternal destination.

CHAPTER 8

THE SPIRIT WORLD IS REAL

"For we wrestle not against flesh and blood, but against principalities, against powers, against the rulers of the darkness of this world". Ephesians 6:12

BREAKING SUICIDAL THOUGHTS

We live in a world where what is seen often dominates what is believed, yet Scripture unveils a different reality: "the things which are seen are temporary, but the things which are not seen are eternal." The invisible realm is not a fantasy, it is the superior reality, shaping the physical world and influencing the minds, emotions, and destinies of people daily. The unseen dimension is not distant or inactive; it surrounds every living soul, full of movement, intelligence, and warfare.

In this realm, every thought can be a signal, every emotion a spiritual echo, every heaviness or sudden lightness a reflection of unseen influence. Depression, despair, and suicidal urges often begin not as random psychological states but as whispers from a darker world. The mind becomes the battleground where invisible forces compete for attention and agreement. When someone begins to feel the unexplainable weight of hopelessness or encounters persistent mental torment, it is often the symptom of invisible manipulation.

Angels and demons coexist in this layered reality, influencing human consciousness in subtle and profound ways. Scripture reveals that even Daniel's prayer was delayed because of unseen opposition (Daniel 10:12. 13). What makes that passage powerful is not just that spiritual beings exist, but that they can resist, delay, or influence human outcomes. Likewise, demonic entities seek to influence mental states, amplifying fear, exhaustion, or despair, while angelic forces strive to sustain hope, courage, and divine strength.

The suicidal mind, in particular, becomes a high-value target for spiritual warfare. Demons of self-hatred and despair aim to isolate the soul from divine light, whispering lies such as "you are worthless" or "no one cares." These are not just negative thoughts; they are spiritual strategies, attempts to disconnect a person from the sustaining presence of God. Many people who have survived suicide attempts describe feeling as though something was "pressing on them," an invisible darkness that felt alive and intelligent. That experience is not imaginary; it is spiritual oppression manifesting in the mind.

Yet just as darkness presses, light also intervenes. God sends His angels to minister to those who are heirs of salvation (Hebrews 1:14). They are active, guarding, guiding, and influencing toward life. Every time a thought of hope rises up, every moment a person feels inexplicably comforted, it is often the result of unseen help. Heaven and hell are both interested in your mind, for the mind is the gateway of dominion. Whichever world you agree with gains authority to act through you.

The Laws That Govern the Invisible World

The invisible world is structured, organized, and governed by spiritual laws. Thoughts of faith and truth attract divine energy; thoughts of despair and deception attract demonic energy. This is why the battle for mental health is not merely medical or emotional, it is profoundly spiritual. If you align with truth, you draw in light. If you agree with lies, you empower darkness. The human soul is like a radio receiver, tuning to frequencies of heaven or hell through meditation, speech, and belief.

Recognizing this reality changes how we respond to inner pain. Instead of surrendering to depression as "who I am," one begins to discern, "this is not me, this is warfare." That discernment alone is deliverance. The moment you see your struggle as a battleground, you are no longer a victim of your thoughts but a soldier with authority over them. The spirit world is real, but you are not helpless within it. Through the power of Christ, you can resist darkness, invite light, and shift atmospheres around you.

Dreams, visions, and deep spiritual impressions are not figments of imagination; they are intersections where the visible and invisible realms touch. The Bible is full of accounts where God or angels communicated through dreams, from Joseph in Egypt to Daniel in Babylon. But just as heaven can speak in the night, so can darkness attempt to invade the same channel. When people experience nightmares of falling, suffocation, or overwhelming darkness, it may not always be psychological disturbance, sometimes, it is evidence of spiritual interference.

Many individuals who wrestle with suicidal impulses recount moments when they felt watched or pressured by an unseen presence. In truth, despair has a personality. Hopelessness is not merely an emotion, it is a spirit. It comes subtly, whispering that life is meaningless, that rest can only come through escape. And once that lie is accepted, it grows stronger. The enemy never forces; he persuades. He presents hopelessness as relief, then turns relief into ruin.

The unseen world is sensitive to agreement. The moment a person agrees with a lie, a doorway opens. This is why Scripture urges, "Do not give place to the devil." Every thought of despair tolerated becomes an entry point for spiritual heaviness. In contrast, every declaration of truth, even whispered through tears, invites angels of comfort and light. The realm around you responds to your internal alignment. What you focus on becomes your atmosphere.

Those who have encountered the spirit world often describe it as more real than this physical one. Some near-death experiences reveal people watching their lifeless bodies from above, fully conscious and aware, even before being revived. Others testify of intense peace or dreadful darkness, depending on the spiritual side they aligned with in life. These accounts may differ in detail, but they all affirm one truth: consciousness continues beyond the brain, because the spirit lives beyond the body.

Despair deepens when the spiritual senses are blinded. A person consumed by darkness may believe no one hears their cry, yet in the unseen world, angels still stand by, and heaven still listens. The tragedy is that pain can drown perception. It is not that help is absent, but that the mind has tuned to a lower frequency. That is why renewing spiritual sensitivity becomes essential. When you reawaken awareness of God's nearness, the darkness loses its power to isolate.

The balance between light and darkness operates on spiritual principles, not emotions. Darkness cannot dwell where light is maintained. Depression thrives in unguarded atmospheres, environments saturated with negative speech, violent media, or unresolved grief. Just as mold grows in moisture, demonic influence grows in emotional and spiritual neglect. Yet when you cultivate praise, truth, and gratitude, light multiplies. The very energy of heaven fills the space around you.

Light and darkness are not abstract ideas; they are living forces. Every thought either increases one or empowers the other. Thoughts of hope, forgiveness, and gratitude strengthen light; thoughts of bitterness and regret fortify darkness. The key to breaking invisible oppression lies in daily alignment, deliberately turning toward truth, choosing to believe the promises of God even when emotions scream otherwise.

The unseen realm responds to divine authority. When you say, "In the name of Jesus, I reject despair and invite peace," those words do not evaporate; they reverberate through the spiritual atmosphere. Angels act upon words of faith just as demons act upon words of fear. This is why prayer is not a weak act of religion but a forceful declaration that reorders realms. It establishes dominion, reminding darkness that it has no ownership of your mind or emotions.

There are unseen wars being fought over every soul, battles for thought, purpose, and destiny. But when you recognize the authority given to you through Christ, you begin to shift from victim to victor. Awareness is deliverance; discernment is protection. Once you understand that the spirit world is not imaginary but interactive, you start to live intentionally, keeping your spiritual space clear, your thoughts anchored, and your heart full of divine light.

Reflection Questions

1. When you think about your own thoughts and emotions, do you ever notice how they might be influenced by something beyond what you can see or explain?

2. How does recognizing the existence of an unseen spiritual reality change the way you understand depression, fear, or despair?

3. What moments in your life have felt like unseen help or comfort reached you when you needed it most?

4. Are there patterns of thought or environments that seem to drain your peace and hope, and how might you begin to guard your mind against them?

5. What daily actions or beliefs could help you align more consistently with peace, truth, and emotional stability instead of hopelessness or fear?

Key Takeaways

- The invisible world is real and active. Thoughts, emotions, and inner battles are often influenced by unseen forces, whether positive or negative.

- Despair is not always psychological alone. Feelings of hopelessness can be symptoms of deeper spiritual pressure or manipulation.

- Light intervenes: Hopeful thoughts, comfort, and moments of peace are often signs of unseen help working to preserve and guide you.

- Your agreement matters: What you choose to believe or focus on determines which influences gain strength in your life, truth empowers peace, lies empower despair.

- Awareness is empowering: Understanding that your struggles may have spiritual roots allows you to respond with intentional thought, care, and self-awareness instead of helplessness.

PART III

THRESHOLDS, REALMS AND THE ILLUSION OF ESCAPRE

CHAPTER 9

SUICIDE AND THE DECEPTION OF PEACE

"There is a way that seems right to a man, but its end is the way of death.". Proverbs 14:12

BREAKING SUICIDAL THOUGHTS

There is a strange silence that often precedes destruction, a deceptive stillness that convinces the weary soul that ending life will finally bring rest. Yet, this silence is not peace; it is the numbing hand of darkness that quiets conviction so that the final blow may fall unresisted. Many who approach suicide describe a sudden calmness before the act, a sense that all torment has lifted. But what they do not realize is that this false calm is not healing, it is spiritual sedation, the anesthetic of hell.

The enemy often withdraws his torment at the final stage so that the soul, deceived into thinking peace has come, may walk willingly into eternal ruin. The spirit of suicide does not kill through pain alone; it kills through false comfort. It convinces the afflicted that death is rest and that peace can be found in escape. But in truth, that peace is a lie, for the peace of suicide is not the peace of God, it is the silence of separation from Him.

The peace of God does not lead to death; it calls to life. It may quiet the storm, but it never destroys the vessel. The enemy mimics that quietness to lead the hopeless into eternal torment. Suicide therefore is not merely an act of despair, it is an act of deception.

The deception of peace in suicide is ancient. The serpent that whispered to Eve still whispers today, "You shall not surely die." He convinces the wounded that life is unbearable and death is relief. He shows the grave as a bed of comfort, not as a prison of regret. But Jesus said, "The thief comes only to steal, to kill, and to destroy." Suicide fulfills that trinity of destruction, it steals hope, it kills destiny, and it destroys eternity.

The so-called relief that follows suicidal thoughts is not the mercy of God, it is the devil's final bait. The moment a person decides to die, the tormenting spirits step aside and allow a deceptive tranquility to enter. That stillness feels divine but is deadly. It is the counterfeit of grace. It is the calm of execution before the judgment seat.

The true peace of Christ carries no guilt, no fear, no darkness. It restores, not ruins. It breathes light, not darkness. If the peace one feels pushes them away from prayer, away from repentance, and away from the will to live, then it is not peace from God but from the enemy.

When Darkness Imitates Light

Satan's most dangerous weapon has always been imitation. He transforms himself into an angel of light to convince men that what is killing them is healing them. Just as he gave Eve a forbidden fruit that appeared good for food but produced death, he now gives the weary heart a forbidden rest that appears good for peace but births destruction.

He copies the language of the Holy Spirit but removes the life from it. He offers a counterfeit mercy that ends in judgment. The deception of suicide, therefore, is not merely emotional, it is deeply spiritual. It presents itself as mercy but ends in wrath. It looks like relief but conceals eternal bondage.

Many who have survived suicide attempts testify that a strange clarity or calm filled their minds moments before they acted. That clarity was not freedom, it was the enemy's silence before slaughter. It was hell's pause to let them step willingly into its gates. The devil's craft is not to frighten but to fascinate. He seduces the hopeless with a false serenity so that they may walk smiling into destruction.

BREAKING SUICIDAL THOUGHTS

In a world that glorifies self-escape, the message of endurance sounds cruel. People say, "If God loves me, why does He not take away the pain?" But love does not always take away pain, it gives purpose to pain. The cross was not the absence of suffering; it was the redemption of suffering. Jesus did not escape death; He conquered it. That is divine mercy.

Suicide promises mercy through death, but God's mercy gives strength to live. Suicide ends the battle; God's mercy wins it. The lie of the enemy is that death is deliverance, but the truth of God is that deliverance is found in life through Christ.

Every voice that whispers, "End it, you will be free," is a voice speaking from beneath the altar of rebellion. Freedom is not found in fleeing life but in surrendering it to the One who gave it. When Elijah prayed to die, God did not grant his request; instead, He fed him, strengthened him, and sent him back to his assignment. Divine mercy restores purpose, it does not terminate it.

Behind every suicidal impulse lies a throne of manipulation. Spirits of despair work in alliance with spirits of deception to fabricate a false narrative of relief. They attack through thoughts, memories, and imaginations, convincing the mind that there is no reason to continue. Then, at the final stage, they step back and allow the illusion of peace to descend.

This spiritual system mirrors how the serpent deceived Eve, first by distortion, then by disobedience, and finally by death. The order never changes. The enemy must first distort the truth of God's goodness, then convince the heart to rebel against His word, and then push the soul toward destruction. Suicide is the climax of that rebellion, the moment a person agrees with the enemy's version of mercy.

But the covenant of life in Christ rejects such deception. The blood of Jesus speaks a better word than despair. It declares that life, not death, is the pathway to peace. The moment a person aligns with the truth of Christ, that spiritual engineering collapses, and the illusion loses its power.

The War Between Voices

The battle around suicide is not merely psychological, it is governmental. It is a war between the voice of despair and the voice of destiny. Every life carries a sound in the Spirit, and the enemy's goal is to silence that sound. When he cannot corrupt it, he tries to stop it. That is why those called to greatness often face intense suicidal attacks, their voice is a threat to darkness.

The enemy fears the voice of testimony. Each time a soul overcomes despair, the kingdom of darkness loses credibility. Hell thrives on silence, but heaven advances through confession. Therefore, the war is about which voice will prevail. Will it be the whisper of death or the declaration of life?

God still asks as He did in Eden, "Who told you?" Who told you that your life is worthless? Who told you that peace can be found in death? The answer to those questions exposes the serpent every time. For the Father of Lights does not speak condemnation into His creation. He calls every life into purpose, not oblivion.

At the heart of redemption is a covenant, a divine promise that those who are in Christ will live and not die but declare the works of the Lord. This covenant is sealed by blood, not by emotion. When a person contemplates suicide, they are unknowingly rejecting that covenant of life for a covenant of deception. But Jesus' blood still speaks louder than that deception.

BREAKING SUICIDAL THOUGHTS

The cross stands as the eternal contradiction to suicide. It proves that pain is not the end, that suffering can be redeemed, and that death is not deliverance but transition into glory. The cross turns despair into destiny. The same blood that cried for mercy on Calvary now cries for every suicidal soul, saying, "Live again."

The lie of suicide loses its strength when exposed to truth. Darkness cannot survive in the presence of revelation. Every suicidal thought is built on a false assumption, that life is meaningless, that suffering is endless, and that peace can only be found beyond the grave. But when the light of God's Word shines, those assumptions crumble.

The Word declares, "You shall know the truth, and the truth shall make you free." The truth does not deny pain, it defines it. Pain is not punishment; it is often the pathway to transformation. God uses pressure to purify purpose. The fire that feels unbearable is often the furnace where destiny is forged.

The enemy lies because he fears the emergence of divine purpose. He knows that the moment truth enters a heart, his deception loses its grip. Every time a person rejects the thought of suicide and chooses to live, a spiritual government collapses. A territory is reclaimed, and a testimony is born. Heaven rejoices not only over the saved soul but over the surviving soul, the one who refuses to die before their destiny is complete.

Even in the deepest despair, the voice of the Lord still calls. It may sound faint, hidden beneath the noise of fear and pain, but it never disappears. Elijah heard that voice not in the wind, nor in the earthquake, nor in the fire, but in a still small whisper. That whisper said, "What are you doing here?"

The same question echoes today: What are you doing here, in this cave of hopelessness, in this valley of despair? The whisper of God does not condemn; it invites. It calls the broken to return to the altar. It calls the weary to drink again from the river of life. It calls every soul entangled by the deception of death to come back to the covenant of life.

The voice of God restores what despair has stolen. It awakens the memory of purpose. It reminds the soul that pain is temporary, but covenant is eternal. The still small voice is not weak, it is sacred. It carries the authority to dismantle the darkness that speaks louder.

The Return to the Altar

Freedom begins at the altar. The altar is not merely a place of sacrifice but a place of exchange, where death is traded for life, and despair for hope. When the soul kneels before the altar, the deception of peace through suicide loses its dominion.

The altar restores alignment. It resets spiritual order. It calls heaven to bear witness that the covenant of life still stands. At the altar, the voice of the accuser is silenced, and the blood of Jesus speaks louder. The altar does not erase pain; it redeems it. It turns what was once a symbol of defeat into a testimony of divine power.

The enemy wants the broken to flee from the altar, to run from prayer, to isolate themselves from the light. But the altar is where life begins again. Every suicidal soul needs not an escape, but an encounter. The encounter breaks the lie and restores vision.

To live beyond the deception of suicide, one must dwell in an atmosphere of life. Atmospheres are spiritual climates that determine what thoughts thrive and what voices prevail. A person surrounded by voices of despair will breathe in hopelessness; one surrounded by the Word of God will breathe life.

Worship changes atmosphere. Prayer cleanses atmosphere. Fellowship strengthens atmosphere. Depression thrives in isolation, but revelation thrives in communion. God designed the church not as a social institution but as a spiritual ecosystem where life multiplies. In the company of believers, despair cannot reign for long.

The enemy's first tactic is to separate the wounded from the body, to whisper, "No one understands you." But the truth is that the body of Christ was designed to carry one another's burdens. Healing flows where unity stands. The atmosphere of life is maintained by obedience, humility, and consistent alignment with truth.

When truth enters, darkness has no negotiation rights. The dominion of light is absolute. That is why the enemy fears revelation. He does not fear emotion; he fears illumination. Once the eyes of the heart are enlightened, suicide loses its mystery. The illusion of peace vanishes, and the soul sees clearly that what appeared as mercy was a masquerade of murder.

The dominion of light restores clarity. It breaks the cycles of emotional instability by anchoring the mind in divine reality. The truth is this: You were created for dominion, not destruction. Every breath you take carries a divine assignment. Every tear you shed waters the ground of purpose. The fact that you are still alive is evidence that God is not finished with you.

Reflection Questions

1. What is the difference between the peace of God and the false peace that often follows suicidal thoughts?

2. How can recognizing the voice of truth help dismantle the deception of suicide?

3. In what ways does returning to the altar restore purpose and realign your soul?

4. What spiritual practices help you maintain an atmosphere of life in your daily walk?

5. How can the revelation of light destroy the dominion of suicidal deception in your mind?

Key Takeaways

- The enemy's calmness before death is a counterfeit of divine stillness.

- The altar is the meeting point where deception dies and truth lives.

- Pain can be redeemed when surrendered to the covenant of life.

- The voice of the Lord still calls every broken soul to live again.

- Light always wins; the dominion of truth is final.

CHAPTER 10

THE BOUNDARY BETWEEN LIFE AND DEATH

"Or ever the silver cord be loosed, or the golden bowl be broken... then shall the dust return to the earth as it was: and the spirit shall return unto God who gave it.". Ecclesiastes 12:6. 7

BREAKING SUICIDAL THOUGHTS

There is a divine line drawn between the worlds of the living and the dead. It is not a wall but a veil, thin enough for the soul to sense, yet strong enough to protect. Scripture reveals that man is a triune being: spirit, soul, and body. The body anchors us to the physical realm, the soul expresses our personality and emotions, and the spirit is the God-breathed essence that gives us life. When that breath departs, the body returns to dust, and the spirit journeys back to God. Between these two realms, flesh and spirit. God placed something mysterious and sacred: the silver cord.

The "silver cord" mentioned by Solomon is more than poetic imagery. It is a spiritual reality, an invisible lifeline woven by the Creator Himself. Through it, the soul of man is tethered to the body, sustained by divine energy and consciousness. It is heaven's umbilical cord, connecting our earthly vessel to the breath of God. As long as the silver cord remains intact, life flows. When it is loosed, death occurs. This is why even in medical emergencies, when someone "comes back" from the edge of death, it is as if that cord was stretched but not severed.

Every heartbeat, every breath, every spark of awareness in your mind is evidence that the silver cord is still intact. Life is not random electricity; it is divine continuity. It means God is still giving you a chance, still holding your soul close to His mercy. That cord is His signature over your existence.

There are moments when life feels unbearable, when pain, shame, rejection, or trauma crushes the soul to the point where death looks like peace. You may have thought, *If only I could leave this world, I would finally rest.* That thought does not make you evil; it makes you human. Pain can twist perception until escape looks holy. But here lies the cruel deception: the voice that tells you to end your life is never God's voice. It is the whisper of demonic forces, ancient deceivers who understand what happens when a person severs their silver cord.

Those forces know that once the cord is cut, there is no coming back. Suicide is not freedom; it is finality. The soul does not drift into peaceful sleep but steps into the realm of spirits, a dimension alive with angels, yes, but also filled with forces of darkness that war against everything God loves. The same voices that said "end it all" are the first to mock and torment the soul that obeyed them. They offer comfort as bait but deliver captivity as consequence.

The pain of this world can feel endless, but it is still temporal. The momentary sufferings of this present world are incomparable to the glory that can still be revealed in you (Romans 8:18). The silver cord is God's mercy cord, a chance to fight another day, to heal, to forgive, to rebuild. To break it by your own hand is to reject the very bridge that could carry you into your next season of redemption.

The Mystery of Out-of-Body Experiences

Across generations, people have described experiences of leaving their bodies, what many call "astral projection" or "out-of-body experiences." Some report floating above themselves, traveling to other realms, or meeting other beings. These experiences, though often described as fascinating or enlightening, touch something sacred and dangerous: the interface between the human soul and the unseen realm.

When one "projects," intentionally or accidentally, they are essentially stretching the silver cord. The soul ventures beyond its God-ordained boundary while the body lies still, tethered only by that invisible line. Those who do this repeatedly open gateways they cannot fully control. The spirit world is not a playground. It is a battlefield populated by both angels and forces of darkness. Every step outside the covering of divine instruction invites interference.

Many who experiment with astral projection encounter beings that radiate light or peace, yet these are not always angels of God. Scripture warns that "Satan himself masquerades as an angel of light." These evil spirits disguise themselves as guides, ancestors, or teachers. They flatter the seeker with illusions of control, but their goal is seduction, to lead the soul away from dependence on God. They promise revelation but deliver bondage. Some who have practiced astral travel for years describe sudden paralysis, night terrors, or unseen attacks upon their sleeping bodies. These are not hallucinations; they are the consequences of tampering with the borders of divine order.

Death occurs when the silver cord is "loosed," as Scripture says. But when it is deliberately severed, through suicide, occult practice, or reckless tampering, something catastrophic happens in the unseen. The soul is violently detached from its earthly vessel. There is no graceful departure, no peaceful glide. It is a spiritual rupture. The soul, unanchored and unprepared, is thrust into realms of spiritual conflict.

Those who commit suicide often find themselves in the company of the very demons that convinced them to end their lives. The voice that whispered "You will finally be free" becomes the voice of accusation and despair. The realm they enter is not rest but reckoning, a space where they encounter the weight of deception they believed. It is a sobering truth: the being that persuades a person to cut the silver cord is the same being that greets them when the cord is cut.

This is why the mercy of God labors so earnestly to keep the cord unbroken. Each sunrise is God saying, *I still want you alive.* Every breath is heaven's vote for your purpose. The pain you feel is not proof that you are abandoned, it is proof that you are still being fought for.

Behind the silver cord is not magic, but mercy. It is God's power sustaining human life through invisible means. Scientists can trace electrical signals, brain waves, and heart rhythms, but they cannot measure the breath of God that sustains them. You are not alive because of biology alone; you are alive because God wills it so.

If you could see the spiritual dimension for one moment, you would understand that you are surrounded by angels who guard that sacred connection between your body and soul. They stand watch as you sleep, ensuring the continuity of life. There are nights you might have died, through sickness, accident, or even your own despair, but something invisible kept you. That something was the cord, and that cord is tied to God's promise that your story is not finished.

Astral projection, occult practices, and suicidal impulses all share one root temptation: the desire to escape pain without surrendering to God. It is the same lie whispered in Eden. "You can have power apart from Him." But the truth is, every attempt to exit the body outside God's timing is rebellion against the Creator's order. Whether through occult projection or self-destruction, both attempt to force a doorway that only God has the key to open.

The silver cord is sacred. It is the divine limit between realms. To meddle with it is to touch what belongs to eternity. To break it is to declare independence from the One who breathed life into you, and that is why the consequences are eternal.

The Cry of God's Heart

Perhaps you are reading these words while battling thoughts of suicide. Perhaps life feels empty and meaningless. You may feel unseen, unheard, and unloved. But hear this truth: you are still connected to God. The silver cord still holds. It has not been cut. The very fact that you can read and breathe means heaven has not given up on you.

God is closer than your next heartbeat. He is not ashamed of your pain. He weeps with you. He sits beside you in the dark room and says, *I know.* He knows how the betrayal felt. He knows the loneliness. He knows the guilt. And still, He says, *Stay.* Stay because redemption is on its way. Stay because light always finds those who refuse to die in the dark. Stay because what feels like the end is only the breaking of your old life, not the ending of your purpose.

The same God who tied your soul to your body through the silver cord can heal the wounds that made you want to cut it. You don't have to understand everything; you only have to hold on.

Think of this: when Jesus hung on the cross, the breath of life was leaving Him, yet He did not take His own life. He yielded it. "Father, into Your hands I commit My spirit." The silver cord was not cut by despair but released in surrender. That is the difference between destruction and redemption. When you surrender your life to God, He doesn't sever your cord. He strengthens it. He turns pain into purpose, wounds into wisdom, and despair into destiny.

As long as the silver cord holds, life can still be rewritten. Healing is still possible. Purpose is still real. The demonic voices that say "End it now" can be silenced by one whisper from Jesus saying, *Live.*

Curiosity has always drawn humanity toward the unknown. From ancient mystics to modern seekers, people have long attempted to pierce the veil separating the physical from the spiritual. Astral projection, lucid travel, and out-of-body exploration have been presented as gateways to enlightenment, a supposed way to "see the unseen" without dying. But beneath the language of discovery lies a grave spiritual risk. What many call "exploration" is often intrusion into realms governed by laws they neither understand nor control.

Those who practice astral projection claim that the soul can temporarily detach from the body, travel beyond the earth, and return when the experience ends. They feel the strange tug of the silver cord, the invisible thread that keeps them from total separation. Yet few realize how dangerous this is. Each time a person deliberately exits their body, they tug at the very cord that was meant to remain untouched until God Himself loosens it. It is like a child playing with the wiring of a live electric current. It might not kill you immediately, but it exposes you to fatal energy.

When the soul leaves the body without divine authorization, it enters a realm already filled with activity, not neutral energy but living presence. There are angels, messengers of light who serve God's purposes, and there are demonic forces, rebellious spirits who thrive on deception and fear. To step into their territory without divine covering is like walking barefoot into a storm of lightning. You may think you are controlling the journey, but you are only a visitor among powers far stronger and older than you.

The Realm Beyond the Veil

Those who have experienced astral projection often describe vivid encounters, floating through walls, hearing voices, seeing landscapes not of this world, and meeting "beings of light." Some even say these entities give them messages, show them future events, or reveal secret knowledge. But not all light is holy. The Apostle Paul warned that "Satan himself transforms into an angel of light." These evil spirits imitate the beauty of divine illumination to seduce the human soul into pride, independence, and curiosity without obedience.

One who ventures into that realm may meet a being that calls itself a guide or protector. It may speak softly, offer wisdom, or even quote Scripture. Yet if that voice draws you away from the name and authority of Jesus Christ, it is not of God. Those entities are masters of mimicry. They flatter the seeker's hunger for meaning, promising enlightenment while leading them further from truth. Many who practiced astral projection for long seasons began to experience spiritual oppression, voices they could not silence, sleep paralysis, nightmares, or an increasing sense of dread when alone.

These manifestations are not the product of imagination. They are the consequence of contact. The demonic forces that inhabit those layers of the unseen thrive on open doors. Every voluntary projection becomes a portal, an invitation written in the language of curiosity. And once the invitation is sent, it is difficult to retract. That is why many find it impossible to stop. The sensations become addictive, the encounters thrilling, yet the aftermath grows darker with time.

Now imagine what happens when, instead of temporarily projecting, a person commits suicide. Astral projection may stretch the cord; suicide severs it. The departure becomes irreversible. The body is left lifeless, the cord snapped, and the soul thrust fully into that same realm it once visited only in part.

In that moment, the person meets the reality behind the whispers, the demons that lured them into hopelessness. What was once a subtle voice becomes a visible presence. The spirit encounters the entities that deceived them into believing that death would bring peace. But peace does not belong to rebellion; it belongs to reconciliation. The same deceivers that whispered comfort now reveal their cruelty. There are testimonies from near-death experiences where individuals felt themselves pulled toward terrifying darkness, surrounded by mocking presences, until they cried out to God for mercy and were revived. Those are glimpses of the truth, that the spirit world is not neutral, and choices on earth determine the alignment of what meets us there.

When the silver cord breaks, the soul becomes visible to the spiritual realm. Angels and demonic forces both perceive its arrival. Angels move according to divine assignment, welcoming those reconciled to God through Christ into rest and light. Demonic forces, however, swarm toward those unshielded by divine covering. They are not simply monsters of horror; they are legalistic beings who claim rights through deception and sin. Suicide gives them a claim because it agrees with their rebellion, it is the rejection of life, the image of God in man.

This is why many ancient accounts of suicide describe torment rather than peace. The soul, having believed the lie, awakens to find the same darkness it tried to escape. The pain it fled has not disappeared; it has transformed. The being that whispered "You'll finally rest" now accuses: "You belong to me." The soul feels naked, cut off, searching for the body it abandoned but unable to return. It is a spiritual homelessness, a state never intended by God.

In contrast, those who experience near-death encounters but are sent back often describe the presence of light and peace, sometimes hearing voices of angels, sometimes seeing glimpses of Jesus. Their cord was stretched but not severed. Their time had not yet come. God, in His mercy, allows such experiences to awaken gratitude and purpose. He gives them a second chance. But those who cut the cord themselves bypass mercy's door and step into judgment unprepared.

There are legitimate spiritual experiences initiated by God, visions, dreams, revelations, and divine encounters. In Scripture, prophets and apostles were sometimes caught up in the Spirit or shown heavenly realities. The difference is *who initiated it.* When God draws a person upward, it is revelation; when a person forces themselves upward, it is trespass. Astral projection is spiritual trespassing. Suicide is spiritual rebellion. Both operate outside divine permission, though one is temporary and the other eternal.

The silver cord was not created for man to control. It was placed as a boundary, a line that keeps order between realms. Every time someone tampers with that boundary, they challenge God's authority. The demonic realm celebrates such defiance because it mirrors their own rebellion against heaven. That is why these experiences often escalate, what begins as curiosity becomes obsession, and what began as fascination ends in torment.

The Mercy in the Cord

Even when a person attempts suicide and survives, it is not coincidence, it is mercy. The silver cord may have been stretched to its limit, but it did not break. That survival is not failure; it is divine rescue. God's angels often intervene, causing delays, distractions, or miraculous rescues that seem accidental but are actually orchestrated by heaven. That remaining connection is God's silent statement: *I still want you alive.*

The silver cord, therefore, is not merely a symbol of life, it is a symbol of divine patience. It represents the thousands of unseen interventions that keep you breathing. When you wake up after wanting to die, it is not because you were strong; it is because heaven refused to let go. The cord still holds because love still holds.

Many who have battled despair believe that death will bring relief, a release from the weight of suffering. That thought often comes as a whisper, subtle and persistent, and it feels convincing because pain clouds discernment.

The truth, revealed to survivors and to those who resist, is starkly different. Death does not deliver peace. What feels like a path to rest is in reality an entry into a realm fraught with forces of darkness that are very real and very intent on keeping the soul away from God's purpose. Those who walk too close to the edge, who even flirt with the idea of severing the silver cord, are met with illusions that masquerade as comfort, beauty, or relief. These are not neutral; they are deceptive encounters designed to lure the soul into despair.

Survivors often recount that the moment they considered ending their life, they sensed a presence, a push toward the act, a feeling that it would finally end the pain. They later realize that this "encouragement" was never from God. It was a demonic trick, a cunning plan of the enemy to convince them to surrender what is sacred. The silver cord, the divine tether holding the spirit to life, is sacred, and any attempt to sever it outside God's timing invites conflict with unseen powers that the human mind cannot comprehend.

BREAKING SUICIDAL THOUGHTS

Those who attempt to tamper with the boundary of life, whether through suicidal thoughts, attempts, or spiritual experiments like astral projection, sometimes encounter realms that are entirely unexpected. These realms are populated by entities, some radiant, some commanding, some frightening, whose motives are not always evident. Survivors describe a profound shock upon realizing that what they imagined as peaceful or freeing was neither.

They may perceive spaces of light, but the light is deceptive, carefully designed by dark forces to appear comforting. Others may encounter demons of confusion, entities that speak in riddles or imitate human voices. The lesson is sobering: the human soul, when untethered from the body without divine permission, becomes vulnerable to spiritual influence. What they thought would be freedom is actually exposure. The silver cord protects, and severing it, whether through suicidal intent or reckless spiritual exploration, removes that protection.

For those who survive attempts on their own life, the aftermath is often marked by profound gratitude and realization. They remember the moments when death seemed like a doorway to peace and see now that it was deception. The voices that encouraged them, the "comfort" that seemed to beckon, were demons, not salvation.

This recognition is painful but also transformative. Survivors often speak of a deep, heart-level awakening: they understand how precious life truly is, how fragile yet protected their soul has been, and how close they were to a permanent loss of purpose. The regret is not shame alone; it is a deep recognition that what they thought would end pain would have only led them further from the mercy and grace of God.

Many describe a sense of relief akin to returning from a perilous journey, a gratitude so intense it reshapes their perspective. Every breath becomes sacred. Every sunrise feels like a personal gift. The cords of life that they once underestimated now appear golden in their understanding, lifelines that they can never take for granted again.

The Reality of Spiritual Influence

One of the hardest lessons survivors learn is that the forces at work during these critical moments are real. Demonic forces actively seek to ensnare, deceive, and promote destruction. They prey on loneliness, shame, and hopelessness, exploiting every opportunity to encourage self-destruction. Their methods are subtle, persuasive, and manipulative.

Conversely, God's angels provide guidance, warning, and intervention, but their work is often unseen until the consequences of the encounter are later revealed. The battle is both internal and external: internal, in the sense that the mind and heart must resist the lies; external, because unseen spiritual entities are at work influencing outcomes. Survivors come to see that life itself is sacred, that the silver cord is not merely a biological lifeline, but a divine lifeline imbued with protection, mercy, and purpose.

Those who return from the edge of despair carry a new perspective. They realize that the supposed peace of death is an illusion, a temporary deception created by forces of darkness. Life, even with its suffering, is always the greater gift. Gratitude becomes a central motif in the lives of these survivors, gratitude for the continued tether of the silver cord, gratitude for God's intervention, gratitude for the unseen angels who preserved their spirit.

They no longer see despair as an ultimate solution; they see it as a signal to reach toward divine help. Pain and struggle are reframed as markers pointing toward the mercy of God, opportunities to experience

His closeness, His comfort, and His protection. In a very real sense, surviving such encounters transforms the way a person moves through the world, giving them an awareness of the spiritual realities around them and a commitment to life that is both redemptive and purposeful.

The story of the silver cord is ultimately a story of choice. Each day, each moment, offers the opportunity to recognize the truth of God's sustaining power versus the lies of demonic forces. For those who have flirted with death, the choice to continue living is also the choice to resist deception. It is a declaration that the whispers of despair will not control destiny.

Life itself becomes an act of spiritual warfare, a daily affirmation that the cord connecting body and soul is sacred, untouchable, and protected by heaven. Every moment lived in gratitude, every act of trust in God, every step toward hope strengthens that tether. Those who once considered severing it come to realize that life is more precious than they ever imagined, and that God's protection and angelic intervention are constant, even when invisible.

Ultimately, the experiences near the edge of despair, whether through suicidal thoughts, attempts, or encounters with spiritual realms, serve as profound lessons. They teach that death is not the solution, that the peace promised by demons is an illusion, and that life preserved by God's mercy is filled with purpose and meaning. Survivors often become advocates of hope, ministers of encouragement, and witnesses to the reality of God's love in moments when despair seemed strongest.

The silver cord, once merely a symbol, becomes a living reminder: your life is tethered by divine will, sustained by God, and protected by His angels. Choosing life is not simply an act of survival, it is an act of worship, obedience, and trust in the One who knows your heart, your pain, and your destiny.

Reflection Questions

1. How has the understanding of the silver cord changed the way you view the value of your life?
2. In what ways have you experienced whispers or thoughts that encouraged despair, and how might you discern their source?
3. How can gratitude and awareness of God's mercy reshape your response to moments of deep pain?
4. What steps can you take to strengthen your connection to life, hope, and divine protection?
5. How might knowledge of spiritual realities, angels, forces of darkness, and the silver cord, influence the choices you make in daily life?

Key Takeaways

- The silver cord is a divine lifeline connecting spirit and body, and it is sacred.
- Suicide or tampering with the cord exposes the spirit to deception and spiritual danger.
- Demonic forces exploit despair, pretending to offer peace while leading toward destruction.
- Angels intervene to protect, guide, and restore those who are vulnerable.

BREAKING SUICIDAL THOUGHTS

- Life, even with suffering, carries purpose and divine potential.
- Gratitude and awareness of God's mercy transform experiences of near loss into spiritual awakening.
- Choosing life is an act of obedience, trust, and spiritual victory over deception.

CHAPTER 11

THE AFTERMATH OF SUICIDE IN THE SPIRIT REALM

And in hell he lift up his eyes, being in torments, and seeth Abraham afar off, and Lazarus in his bosom.". Luke 16:23

Death does not end awareness. It only changes the environment in which the soul exists. When the final breath leaves the body, the spirit does not dissolve, it awakens. The shock of that transition is indescribable, for the person who thought everything would end suddenly realizes that everything continues, only without the body as its vessel. In that moment, clarity floods the soul. Everything once blurred by pain becomes terrifyingly vivid.

Scripture says, "It is appointed unto men once to die, but after this the judgment." (Hebrews 9:27) This means that the moment life on earth ends, the spirit immediately faces the truth of eternity. There are no pauses, no empty voids, no waiting rooms of unconscious rest. The spiritual world begins where physical life stops, a realm of intense reality, where motives, choices, and unseen forces are revealed with absolute transparency. Suicide, which promises escape, therefore opens the soul to the most penetrating truth it has ever encountered.

In that instant, all illusions collapse. The soul realizes that pain cannot be killed, only transferred. The despair that seemed unbearable on earth now stands before divine justice, where motives and deceptions are weighed. The person who believed death would silence suffering discovers that the mind still thinks, the emotions still feel, and the conscience still remembers. What has ended is only the body's ability to choose.

The body was meant to be a temporary garment for the eternal spirit, a house through which divine purpose could be fulfilled. When suicide destroys the body prematurely, it does not destroy the person; it only evicts the soul from its earthly assignment. The spiritual law remains: the soul must face what it has done with the life it was given. This is not because God is cruel, but because truth must be faced before peace can ever be restored.

When Jesus told the story of the rich man and Lazarus in Luke 16, He unveiled a sobering reality: after death, consciousness continues. The rich man, though separated from his body, could see, feel, remember, and regret. He could still desire mercy, but could no longer choose repentance. This illustrates the spiritual aftermath of any death, but especially suicide, which attempts to escape judgment by self-termination. The result is not freedom from judgment, but an immediate encounter with it.

Some people have experienced near-death encounters where they reported intense regret the moment they crossed the threshold. One described it as “a loud realization that I had just violated something eternal.” Another said, “I thought I would find rest, but I entered awareness, not peace.” These testimonies align with Scripture’s portrayal of the spirit realm as a place of heightened consciousness, where motives and realities once hidden are now fully visible.

Revelation After Death

In the aftermath of suicide, there is no longer deception, only revelation. The soul sees the spiritual forces that contributed to its decision, the demonic manipulations, the lies whispered over years, the unseen pressures that distorted perception. There is often an instant understanding that the pain was never meant to destroy them but to draw them toward divine healing. The tragedy is that this realization comes when the opportunity to choose life is gone.

This is not to say that all who die by suicide are instantly condemned. God’s justice is perfectly balanced with mercy. He alone knows the weight of mental anguish, the influence of darkness, and the depth of deception that clouded each person's mind. But the law of spiritual cause and effect still stands: suicide cuts short divine purpose. It interrupts the journey that was meant to lead to healing and redemption. What the enemy could not achieve through despair, he attempts to accomplish through premature death, robbing heaven of destiny.

Yet even here, mercy speaks. Scripture reveals that God's compassion reaches beyond our comprehension. The moment of death is not the end of His heart toward His creation. There are mysteries of grace that human minds cannot fully grasp, divine interventions that occur in the soul's final seconds. For this reason, the living must not sit in judgment, but in urgency, urgency to prevent, to love, and to intercede for those still breathing. For as long as a person lives, the door of mercy remains open.

The spiritual aftermath of suicide is not the end of God's compassion, but it is the end of choice. That is why life is sacred: because it is the only environment where change, repentance, and redemption can occur. In eternity, reality is fixed. Therefore, every day on earth is a chance, a gift from heaven to decide which side of eternity your soul will awaken on. To those who are tired and near the edge, the Spirit of God cries out even now: "Choose life, that you and your descendants may live."

The moment after death is not what most expect. It is not a black void, nor a sleep without dreams. It is awareness, heightened, unfiltered, and absolute. The spirit world is not a distant fantasy but an ever-present dimension, unveiled the instant the soul leaves the body. For those who died in peace with God, that moment is radiant, a surge of light, warmth, and indescribable love. For those who cross the threshold through despair, confusion and regret often take its place. The separation between light and darkness becomes clear, not as punishment, but as truth finally seen without distortion.

In that realm, there are no secrets. Every motive, word, and thought appears before the soul like scenes from a book that has been opened. The Scripture says, "The books were opened... and the dead were judged according to what they had done." (Revelation 20:12) This judgment is not merely about deeds but about alignment, the spiritual direction of the heart. Heaven does not weigh success but surrender. The question becomes: to whom or to what did you give your agreement?

For the person who took their life, the first realization is often that life was never theirs to end. It was entrusted. God is the source and owner of every breath, and our existence is sacred because it reflects His image. The human spirit, made in His likeness, carries an eternal imprint of His essence. To destroy the vessel does not destroy that imprint; it only removes the protective layer that kept it within time. Suddenly exposed to eternity, the soul understands the weight of its decision. It realizes that death was not escape, it was entrance into full awareness.

This awareness is accompanied by the recognition of spiritual laws. The soul understands that every choice carried consequence, every belief created energy, and every moment of despair could have been transformed by truth if accepted. The lies whispered during life. "You are worthless," "God has abandoned you," "There's no way out", are seen for what they were: deceptions crafted by forces that hated the image of God within you. The spirit of suicide is unmasked as a parasite that feeds on human sorrow, offering release while chaining the soul to regret.

At the moment of crossing, spiritual beings await. Angels of light or entities of darkness, not myth, but reality. The Scripture tells us that when Lazarus died, angels carried him to Abraham's bosom. (Luke 16:22) In contrast, the rich man, who had lived without repentance, found himself in torment, aware of his separation from God. The same pattern unfolds for every soul: the realm that governed one's inner world in life now becomes one's dwelling in eternity. Light attracts light, and darkness draws darkness.

Those aligned with despair find themselves surrounded by its echo. They realize that every hopeless thought was a doorway that invited something deeper, a presence, a weight, a voice that wasn't theirs. In death, they see that these whispers came from entities that had watched, waited, and whispered for years, eager to claim a soul separated from faith. This is the harvest of spiritual law: what you continually agree with becomes your companion.

Yet in this somber revelation, mercy is not absent. The mercy of God is like a flame that flickers even in the darkest corners of eternity. There are testimonies of those who were brought back from near-death experiences, who described hearing a voice calling them back before it was too late, a voice filled not with accusation but with sorrowful love. They reported realizing, in those few moments beyond the veil, that the One they thought had forsaken them had been near them all along. The regret that follows such realization is immense, but it becomes a witness to the living: life is the field of choice; death only reveals the harvest.

The aftermath of suicide in the spirit realm is therefore not merely punishment, it is exposure. The soul stands before ultimate truth. There is no more pretending, no hiding behind explanations. The pain that was once psychological becomes spiritual; the fog lifts, and everything that was distorted comes into focus. For some, this clarity brings immediate sorrow, a longing to return, to undo, to reach for the hand they once rejected. But the boundary is fixed. The body was the bridge between time and eternity, and once crossed, the bridge is gone.

However, even in the face of justice, God's mercy remains part of the equation. The Judge is also the Redeemer. Divine justice is not fueled by wrath but by restoration, the restoration of divine order. Judgment does not mean cruelty; it means truth cannot coexist with lies. When the soul faces what it has done, the encounter with truth is both cleansing and piercing. For those who died believing in God but overtaken by despair, mercy still intercedes. Christ, who descended even into death, remains the Advocate who pleads for those deceived by darkness. His blood speaks beyond the grave.

The Danger of Gambling with Grace

But this should not make anyone casual about life. The mysteries of mercy are not excuses to gamble with eternity. To rely on posthumous grace while rejecting present help is spiritual suicide twice over, once in life, and once beyond it. The Bible warns that today is the day of salvation, not tomorrow, not after the act. The living must seize the invitation now, because awareness after death cannot rewrite destiny. The moment to choose life is always now.

For those left behind, understanding this reality is both sobering and healing. It calls them to compassion, not condemnation. The tragedy of suicide is not merely that a life was lost, but that a battle was misunderstood. The person did not simply give up; they were deceived by an intelligent spiritual enemy. Our response should not be judgment but warfare, prayer, awareness, and love that fights for the despairing before they cross that line. Every prayer, every conversation, every moment of listening can become a hand pulling someone back from the edge.

Eternity is not an abstract doctrine; it is a continuation of consciousness. The decisions made in time ripple forever. But so does grace, and grace is the louder sound. As long as breath remains, no lie is final, and no despair is unbreakable. The truth about suicide and the spirit realm is not meant to terrify but to awaken. It shows the immense value of every human life, that you are more than chemicals and pain, that your existence reverberates in realms unseen, that heaven itself mourns at your suffering and fights for your survival.

So if you are reading this and feel like ending your life would bring peace, hear this: it will not. It will only open your eyes to how loved you were, how deceived you became, and how close salvation always stood. Life may be unbearable now, but eternity without chance to choose again is far heavier. The same God who rules eternity is still calling to you in time, not with condemnation, but with the same voice that raised Lazarus from the dead: "Come forth."

You are not too far gone. The aftermath of suicide in the spirit realm is irreversible, but your story is not finished. Heaven still waits for your yes. The air still carries the whisper of mercy. The hand of God still reaches into your darkness, offering peace that restores, not destroys. Choose life, even when it trembles. Because eternity listens to the choice you make today.

Reflection Questions:

1. How do you imagine the spiritual world after death?
2. Does the idea of divine justice bring fear or clarity?
3. What kind of legacy are your current choices creating?
4. How does knowing God's mercy is still available change your outlook?

Key Takeaways:

- Death reveals what life concealed.
- Every choice echoes in eternity.
- Darkness seeks to claim hopeless souls.
- God's justice is balanced by mercy.
- As long as you live, grace can rewrite your ending.

PART IV

DELIVERANCE, RESTORATION, AND BREAKING DEMONIC SOVEREIGNTY

CHAPTER 12

THERE IS STILL TIME AND HOPE

"Behold, now is the accepted time; behold, now is the day of salvation.". 2 Corinthians 6:2

There is a strange heaviness that settles over the soul when hope begins to fade. It's not always loud. Sometimes it's just a dull ache, a sense that the light that once burned inside is dimming, and that no amount of effort seems to reignite it. This is the silent weight that drives many toward the thought of ending it all. It is not that they hate life, it is that they cannot find a way to live with the pain.

If you are reading this, something in you is still reaching. That reach itself is hope. Even if your mind denies it, your soul still believes there is something worth waiting for. You may feel beyond repair, beyond forgiveness, beyond peace, but the truth is, you are not beyond love. The divine does not recoil from your darkness; it leans into it. When Scripture says, "His mercies are new every morning," it is describing a rhythm built into existence. Every sunrise is heaven's silent sermon that yesterday's mistakes did not end your story.

There is a lie that creeps into broken minds, the lie that God is tired of you, that the world would be better without you, that nothing can change. This lie has killed more people than any weapon. It hides behind memories of failure and amplifies the voice of guilt until it feels like a verdict. But guilt is not a verdict; it is an invitation. It means your conscience is still alive, still capable of being restored. The dead do not feel guilt, the living do. And that means there is still room for transformation.

God in the Midst of Pain

You might look at the chaos around you and ask, "Where is God in all this?" He is closer than your next breath. The problem is not absence but interference. Pain is loud, trauma echoes, and despair screams. Yet beneath the noise, there is still a pulse of mercy calling you to breathe one more time. Psalm 34:18 says, "The Lord is close to the brokenhearted and saves those who are crushed in spirit." If your spirit is crushed, then you are exactly where God draws nearest.

Many imagine that divine love is reserved for the strong, the holy, or the healed. But God's love is most intense for the wounded. He sits with the suicidal, weeps with the betrayed, and waits with the abandoned. He is not watching from a distance; He is whispering from within, "Don't quit yet." His love does not erase pain instantly, but it transforms how pain is carried. It gives purpose to survival and dignity to struggle.

If you feel exhausted, it does not mean you are weak. It means you've been fighting battles most people can't see. Your endurance has been invisible to others but not to heaven. Every tear shed in silence is counted, every sleepless night recorded. Even your questioning is a kind of faith, it means you still care enough to ask. The divine can work with questions; what it cannot work with is silence that gives up.

God's love is not exhausted. It is eternal energy, always renewing, always pursuing. "Nothing can separate us from the love of God," Paul wrote, "neither death nor life, angels nor demons, nor any powers, nor anything else in all creation." (Romans 8:38. 39) That means even suicidal thoughts cannot separate you from divine affection. They can cloud it, but they cannot erase it. Love is woven deeper into your being than despair can reach.

Perhaps you've prayed before and felt nothing. That silence was not rejection; it was preservation. Sometimes God does not answer with words because your heart is too raw to receive them. Instead, He wraps you in invisible care, through the stranger who smiles, the friend who texts at the right time, or the inner nudge that says, "Wait." These are not coincidences; they are small resurrections of hope disguised as ordinary moments.

Healing begins not with a miracle, but with a decision: to live one more day. It may not feel holy, but it is one of the most sacred acts of defiance against darkness. When you choose to live, even when you feel nothing, you declare that despair does not own your ending. God writes in chapters, not in single moments. What feels final today may only be a comma in the story of redemption.

If you could see your life from eternity's perspective, you would realize how incomplete your pain's narrative is. You have not yet seen what God can make from the ashes. There are people you have not yet met, joys you have not yet known, purposes you have not yet lived. Despair is impatient, it tells you the story is over when the Author is still writing.

The mind that contemplates death is not evil; it is tired. But weariness can be healed. That is why reaching out is vital. Tell someone. Silence is where despair multiplies. The enemy thrives in isolation because that's where lies echo without resistance. The moment you speak, the darkness loses power. You are not a burden; you are a person fighting unseen wars. The right listener can become a lifeline.

The Power of Asking for Help

Reaching out does not make you weak. It makes you human. Even Jesus needed Simon of Cyrene to carry His cross. If the Son of God accepted help, you can too. Therapy, counseling, prayer groups, trusted friends, these are tools heaven uses to rebuild shattered strength. God works through people. Don't reject His help because it wears human skin.

Sometimes hope doesn't arrive as an explosion of joy, it arrives as a whisper that says, "You're still here." And if you are still here, it means purpose still pulses through your veins. Life is not a punishment; it is a process. Every stage, even the dark ones, serves a purpose in shaping your soul. You are being prepared for something larger than pain. The current storm is not proof of God's absence; it is preparation for resilience.

It is easy to believe the lie that nothing will ever change. But history, and eternity, are filled with people who felt the same and lived to see transformation. The addict who thought they were hopeless and became a counselor. The depressed teenager who survived and now writes songs that heal others. The widow who wanted to die but became a foster mother. Every miracle began with a decision to not give up on the next breath.

Healing is not a single moment; it's a thousand small choices to keep going. Some days you'll walk, some days you'll crawl, and some days you'll only breathe, but that's still movement. And movement is life. The divine does not demand perfection; it celebrates persistence. Even the smallest spark of will is enough for God to ignite restoration.

You are not what happened to you. You are not the mistake you made, nor the rejection you faced. You are a soul in progress, crafted in love, sustained by grace. The world may not understand your depth, but heaven does. The very breath you take now is evidence of that investment. If you could feel what God feels when He looks at you, despair would lose its vocabulary.

The truth is simple but radical: you still have time, and hope still exists. Time means possibility; hope means power. You are not waiting for a distant miracle, you are the miracle still unfolding.

Every heartbeat is a declaration that eternity has not given up on you. You have a future that the darkness is afraid of. That's why it's fighting you so hard. But it will not win, not if you decide to breathe again.

When a person stands on the edge of hopelessness, time seems to dissolve. Moments blur, days drag, and the mind feels suspended between wanting relief and fearing what comes next. But here is the mystery of hope: it can rise again from ashes you thought were too cold to hold life. Hope is not dependent on feelings; it is sustained by truth. Feelings change like tides, but truth remains, you are still loved, still wanted, still redeemable.

There are many who once stood where you stand. They felt the same suffocating weight, the same haunting whisper that said, "There's no way out." Yet today, they breathe freely. What changed for them was not that pain vanished overnight, but that they discovered pain was not their final chapter. The storm they thought would drown them became the rain that grew new life in them.

Sometimes, hope doesn't enter through the front door. It sneaks in through small things, a memory of laughter, a sudden calm in prayer, a stranger's kindness, a child's smile. These are not coincidences. They are signs that light is still breaking through the cracks of despair. Life has a way of sending messages from eternity, whispering, "You still matter."

One of the greatest lies the enemy tells is that suicide will bring peace. But what it actually brings is silence, a silence that halts every possibility of future joy. The pain of this moment is temporary, but the consequences of ending your life are eternal. When Scripture says, "Choose life," it is not a command born of duty, but of mercy.

God knows that even when you can't see how, life will unfold into beauty again.

Even if you have failed many times, even if you've relapsed, fallen, or lost everything, your story is not wasted. In fact, brokenness often becomes the soil where destiny grows best. Every scar becomes a map of redemption. Every weakness becomes a place where God's strength can shine through. The Apostle Paul wrote, "My grace is sufficient for you, for my power is made perfect in weakness." Grace is not just forgiveness, it is energy that restores what despair has drained.

The Warfare of Reaching Out

It's okay to admit that you need help. We were never designed to carry pain alone. The human soul is built for connection, and isolation poisons it. That is why reaching out is not just emotional, it is spiritual warfare. The devil thrives in secrecy; healing thrives in the open. When you speak your pain, you strip darkness of its hiding place. The very act of saying, "I'm not okay," invites heaven into the conversation.

If you feel like you've lost control, remember this: control is not the goal, surrender is. Not surrender to despair, but to divine care. Let God take the weight. You were never meant to bear it alone. Life may not make sense now, but it does not need to for it to still be sacred. You don't have to understand everything to choose hope. You only need to take one step, just one, and heaven will meet you there.

Sometimes, people imagine that God only saves the righteous. But if that were true, none of us would qualify. The cross stands as the eternal reminder that God specializes in lost causes.

The Son of God didn't die for the perfect; He died for the broken, the ashamed, the weary, and the forgotten. If you think you've gone too far, remember the thief on the cross. He had no time left to make amends, yet mercy still found him in his final breath. If there was hope for him, there is surely hope for you.

There are seasons when you will feel numb, where prayer feels mechanical and faith feels dead. Do not interpret that numbness as abandonment. Sometimes numbness is the soul's defense against overload. It's not evidence of failure, it's evidence that you've been through too much for too long. In those moments, let God carry you. Let others pray for you when you can't find words. Healing begins when you allow yourself to be held, even when you feel nothing.

Remember: life is not only about surviving pain; it's about discovering purpose within it. Pain transforms when it finds meaning. You might not see it now, but your struggle could one day become someone else's survival guide. The very darkness that once tried to destroy you could become the light that rescues another. That is how God redeems pain. He turns victims into healers.

You may wonder why God allows suffering. It's a mystery we will never fully grasp, but we know this: He never wastes it. Every tear, every disappointment, every loss. He collects and converts them into something that builds eternal weight in your spirit. The suffering that feels unbearable now may one day become the story that saves someone else's life. And in that moment, you will understand why you had to live through it.

There is a scene in Scripture where Jesus arrives too late, at least, from everyone's perspective. Lazarus was already dead. His sisters said, "If you had been here, my brother would not have died."

But what they called too late, Jesus called the right time. Because the miracle wasn't meant to prevent death, it was meant to prove resurrection. That is your story too. What looks like the end to you might be the setup for your resurrection moment.

You are not finished. You are not forgotten. There are songs left to be sung, stories left to be written, laughter left to be shared. There are mornings ahead where you will wake up and realize that the pain that once ruled you has lost its grip. You will breathe deeply again, and it will not hurt. You will find yourself smiling without forcing it. These moments will come, if you wait, if you breathe, if you stay.

If you ever find yourself at the edge again, whisper this: "I will not end what God is still writing." Say it even when you don't believe it. Words have power. The same breath that once cried in pain can speak life again. Declare that you are not a mistake, that you are not a burden, that you are worth healing. Heaven listens to such declarations with fierce attention.

And when you don't have words, let silence be your prayer. Let your tears speak. Let your heartbeat be your amen. God understands language beyond speech. Every exhale of exhaustion is still worship if it carries the desire to live. You do not need eloquence; you need honesty. Tell God exactly how you feel, even if it's angry, confused, or bitter. He can handle it. What He cannot handle is distance.

The light is coming. It may not be dramatic; it may begin as a small glimmer in your soul. But it will grow. Every act of survival, every moment you refuse to surrender, strengthens that light. It will guide you back to peace, to purpose, to joy. One day you will tell your story, and someone else will find the courage to live because you did. That is how hope multiplies, it is born in pain and blooms in testimony.

You are not alone, not forgotten, and not finished. This life still holds meaning. The night may feel long, but dawn is already on its way. And when it breaks, you will realize what heaven has been trying to tell you all along, there is still time, and there is still hope.

Reflection Questions

1. What lies have you believed about your worth that you can now confront with truth?
2. How might your pain become a source of healing for others one day?
3. What are three small acts of hope you can choose this week?
4. Who can you invite into your journey toward restoration?

Key Takeaways

- You are not too late for redemption or recovery.
- Hope often begins in small, quiet moments.
- Pain can be transformed into purpose.
- God never wastes suffering. He recycles it into testimony.
- The light always returns for those who choose to wait for dawn.

CHAPTER 13

OVERCOMING THE DEMONIC PULL TOWARD SUICIDE

"The law of the Spirit of life in Christ Jesus has set me free from the law of sin and death.". Romans 8:2

BREAKING SUICIDAL THOUGHTS

There are battles no psychiatrist can explain, no therapist can quantify, and no medication can silence. These are the battles waged in unseen realms, where invisible hands press the mind, whispering despair until the soul trembles on the edge of death. This is where the demonic machinery behind suicidal oppression operates: silent, strategic, and relentless. Yet even in this thick darkness, the light of Christ burns hotter than the flames of hell. Deliverance is not a metaphor, it is an encounter.

Every suicide begins as a suggestion. It is not the person who initiates the idea; it is a voice. That voice first knocks lightly, disguised as self-pity, wrapped in logic. *"Maybe everyone would be better without you."* It sounds like your own thought, but it carries a cold intelligence that isn't yours. That is oppression, the stage where demonic spirits hover just outside the human aura, projecting hopeless thoughts into the mind like fiery darts. You resist them, they retreat. You let your guard down, they return. This is the invisible conversation that takes place between the human soul and spirits of despair, rejection, and self-annihilation.

If those thoughts are entertained repeatedly, oppression mutates into obsession. Now the spirit doesn't merely visit, it finds partial lodging in the soul. The person becomes preoccupied with death, darkness, and escape. Every mirror whispers condemnation. Every silence becomes a battlefield. The demon begins to feed on emotional exhaustion. Sleep disappears. Appetite fades. Thoughts loop in endless circles of pain. You are no longer merely being attacked, you are being influenced.

And if this stage is not confronted by truth and power, obsession deepens toward possession. In this final descent, the spirit seizes more control over the will. The voice that once suggested now commands. The person may describe it as "something taking over me." It is here that the demon uses the body to execute its final mission: to destroy the vessel

God intended for glory. Possession is not always dramatic; sometimes it is a calm, calculated surrender of the will to darkness.

But let it be clear, even in the thickest oppression, there is still authority in the name of Jesus Christ. The same voice that raised Lazarus from the grave still pierces the corridors of despair. The power of deliverance begins the moment truth is recognized.

Step 1: Recognition and Confession of the Battle

The first act of deliverance is not prayer, it is awareness. You must recognize that suicidal ideation is not merely psychological; it is spiritual. The moment you call the enemy by name, his disguise is broken. Say out loud: *"This is not me; this is the spirit of death trying to manipulate me."* Hell loses power when you expose its deception.

Step 2: Renunciation of the Lie

Demons feed on agreement. When you echo their words internally. "I'm worthless," "No one cares," "God has abandoned me", you sign invisible contracts. Break those agreements by verbal warfare. Speak the opposite of what you hear. "I am chosen. I am loved. I am alive by divine design." Truth is not emotion; it is ammunition.

Step 3: Repentance and Surrender

Darkness thrives in rebellion, but surrender invites divine jurisdiction. Tell God, *"I give You my will, my pain, my mind."* When you surrender your will, the enemy loses legal ground. Repent for every space where bitterness or unbelief gave him a foothold. The Blood of Jesus does not just forgive sin, it breaks spiritual ownership.

Step 4: Seek Deliverance. Not Just Counseling

Counseling helps the soul reason; deliverance sets the spirit free. You cannot counsel a demon; it must be cast out. Many have sat through endless sessions, learning coping mechanisms while an ancient spirit still sits enthroned in their thoughts. Continue counseling for emotional rebuilding, but also seek an encounter with divine power. Deliverance is not cruelty; it is mercy in motion.

Step 5: Connect with a True Power Carrier

Find a minister who carries fire, not just words. There are preachers who quote Scripture yet tremble before darkness, and there are men and women who live in prayer until their very voice shakes principalities. Seek those who fast, who stay on their knees until chains break. The anointing they carry is not charisma, it is current. Stay under their covering until the fog lifts.

Step 6: Invocation of the Blood and Name of Jesus

The Blood of Jesus is not symbolic poetry; it is legal currency in the spirit realm. When you invoke it, you remind hell of its defeat. Speak the name *"Jesus"* with conviction and desperation. Call until something shifts inside you. Behind the veil, angels mobilize when that name is cried out in faith. You may not see them, but the realm of darkness feels their arrival.

Step 7: Atmosphere Management. Fill Your Space with Worship

Demons suffocate in environments saturated with worship. Music birthed from holy presence carries frequency that repels them. Fill your room with songs that carry glory. Michael W. Smith, Don Moen,

Shane & Shane, voices that invite heaven. Let worship play for hours. Even if you cannot pray, listen and whisper gratitude. As you do, light will begin to invade your atmosphere; the heaviness will break like glass under thunder.

Step 8: Breaking Agreements and Gateways

Every traumatic event, every dark conversation, every secret vow can create an entry point. Say, *"I break every agreement made with death, darkness, and despair."* Name them. If you once said, *"I wish I could die,"* revoke those words. Words are doors. Seal them with the Blood of Jesus.

Step 9: Infilling of the Holy Spirit

Deliverance is not complete until the Holy Spirit occupies the spaces once held by torment. Invite Him deliberately: *"Spirit of God, fill every room of my soul."* When He fills you, He fortifies you. Empty houses attract intruders; filled temples repel them.

Step 10: Mind Renewal through Scripture Meditation

The battlefield is not around you; it is within you. Every verse you meditate on rewires a neural pathway. Replace lies with truth daily. Whisper verses like medicine. "I shall not die, but live." "God has not given me the spirit of fear." These are not clichés; they are spiritual codes that fortify the mind's gate.

Step 11: Community and Accountability

Demons thrive in secrecy. Healing accelerates in community. Find believers who radiate peace, not judgment. Confess your struggles to those who know how to pray, not gossip. Accountability is not control; it is protection.

Step 12: Prophetic Prayer and Word Warfare

Open your mouth and declare: *"I am the temple of the Holy Spirit; no spirit of death has jurisdiction over me."* Decrees establish boundaries in the invisible. The same mouth that once echoed despair must now release decrees of life. Heaven's armies move along the sound of faith.

Step 13: Re-establishment of Purpose

Hopelessness dies where purpose is reborn. Begin to ask, *"Why did God spare me?"* Purpose is the antidote to suicide. The devil cannot destroy what understands its mission. Write down the dreams you buried; they are your recovery map.

Step 14: Maintenance Through Spiritual Discipline

Deliverance must be maintained. Pray even when you don't feel spiritual. Fast to weaken the flesh. Fill your mornings with gratitude. Keep your eyes from dark media, your ears from hopeless talk. Guard your atmosphere like a fortress. Freedom is not a moment, it is a lifestyle.

When these steps are practiced with desperation and consistency, demonic systems crumble. You will begin to feel the atmosphere shift, nightmares will cease, heaviness will lift, peace will start to return. The same demons that whispered destruction will flee at the whisper of *Jesus.*

No matter how deep the pit, the Blood still speaks louder. The voices of hell may roar, but the voice of the Lord still thunders over many waters. The one who was almost destroyed can become a deliverer for others. This is the mystery of divine reversal, when the hunted becomes the hunter, when the captive becomes the chain-breaker.

Deliverance is not the end, it is the beginning of reclamation. The moment the demonic influence is broken, the battle shifts from expulsion to occupation. The empty soul must now be filled, the cleansed vessel must now be guarded, and the renewed mind must be continually fed with light. Freedom is not sustained by emotion; it is sustained by discipline, by vigilance, and by communion with the Holy Spirit.

After liberation, the atmosphere feels lighter, but the enemy will test the gates. He will whisper again, not to possess, but to probe for weakness. His strategy is to see whether the old habits of thought and emotion still provide access. He will bring familiar memories, pain, rejection, failure, and try to reattach the past to your present. This is why maintenance is warfare, not leisure. The heart must become a guarded city, surrounded by walls of truth and patrolled by the Word of God.

The first weapon in sustaining freedom is *daily worship*. Worship creates an environment where God's presence is continually hosted. It is not about music style; it is about atmosphere. The same way toxic sounds invite darkness, sacred melodies invite light. Play worship that carries the fragrance of heaven. Let your home become a sanctuary. When the atmosphere is filled with adoration, demonic activity cannot coexist. Darkness suffocates in the oxygen of praise. Even in silence, whisper thanksgiving. Gratitude is a shield that blocks despair.

Next is *Scripture meditation*. Do not rush through verses; let them speak to you. The mind that was once a playground for intrusive thoughts must now become a garden of divine truth. Repetition rewires the brain; meditation rewires the soul. Memorize verses that proclaim identity, hope, and victory. Say them aloud when fear strikes. "I am God's workmanship." "The Lord is my light and my salvation; whom shall I fear?" "No weapon formed against me shall prosper." Each declaration plants light in the neural pathways once occupied by darkness. The Word of God is both medicine and mirror, it heals and reveals who you truly are.

Thirdly, *establish prayer routines.* Do not wait for emotional motivation to pray. Set fixed times, morning, noon, and night. Consistency invites divine habitation. Prayer is not just talking; it is positioning. Even silent prayer builds spiritual voltage. When you pray in tongues, you strengthen your inner man. When you pray with understanding, you realign your thoughts. Prayer is both weapon and therapy. It ventilates the soul and disarms the enemy. And even when your words feel weak, God interprets the groaning of your heart as incense rising before His throne.

Another key is *deliverance maintenance through holy living.* Freedom must be preserved by purity. Unforgiveness, bitterness, and immoral indulgence reopen old wounds. Keep short accounts with God. Repent quickly when conviction stirs. Holiness is not perfection, it is separation from darkness. Demons thrive where compromise hides. When you walk in light, their darkness disappear. When you close the door of sin, you close the gate of torment.

Then comes community. Isolation is the devil's workshop. The one who stands alone is easily deceived. Find fellowship with believers who carry life. Surround yourself with people who pray, who speak faith, who understand spiritual warfare. Avoid environments saturated with cynicism and doubt. Choose conversations that build. Spiritual growth accelerates in community. Healing happens faster when you are seen, known, and prayed for. The Church is not perfect, but it is a spiritual ecosystem of protection. Within it, faith multiplies, and despair loses its hiding place.

Next, cultivate *fasting and consecration*. Fasting is not punishment, it is purification. It subdues the flesh so that the spirit can ascend. Many invisible chains break during fasting seasons. The appetite of the body often feeds the appetite of the enemy. When you fast, your spiritual senses sharpen. The mind that was once clouded with heaviness becomes clear. The Holy Spirit begins to whisper instructions, corrections, and revelations. Consecration, living intentionally holy and separate, keeps your spirit tuned to the frequency of heaven.

Another vital step is *watchfulness over sensory gates*. What you watch, listen to, and entertain builds your spiritual climate. Avoid content soaked in fear, lust, or violence. These are channels through which oppression reenters. Fill your eyes with Scripture, your ears with worship, and your mouth with confession of truth. The eyes and ears are gates; guard them like sacred portals. Remember: the enemy cannot possess what you do not feed.

Then there is *forgiveness*. Unforgiveness anchors demonic presence. It keeps the soul in emotional captivity. You cannot be free while rehearsing old pain. Forgiveness is not weakness, it is weaponry. When you release others, you also release yourself. It is the tearing down of emotional prisons where bitterness incubates. The moment you forgive, peace begins to flow again, and the Holy Spirit fills the vacuum where resentment once lived.

You must also learn *spiritual discernment*. Not every dream, thought, or feeling is random. Sensitivity to the Spirit allows you to recognize when the enemy is attempting to reattach his cords. When you sense heaviness, confusion, or sudden sadness, do not panic, speak life. Declare, *"The Lord is my light; I refuse this oppression."* Worship immediately. The faster you respond, the weaker the attack becomes. Discernment allows you to strike before the darkness takes root.

Confession and testimony are next. Tell your story. Share your deliverance. The testimony you hide becomes the victory you delay. When you speak of what God has done, it seals the work in your own heart and ignites hope in others. Every time you say, *"God delivered me,"* the echo of your voice builds resistance against relapse. Your testimony is a sword, swing it often.

And finally, *walk in purpose*. Purpose is the oxygen of the soul. When you discover why you exist, suicidal ideation loses its foundation. Begin to serve others. Volunteer, create, mentor, write, build. Every act of giving reestablishes the meaning of your survival. You did not just escape death, you were sent back as a witness. The very area where the devil tried to kill you will become the field of your anointing. What once was a tomb will become a platform.

Freedom is not instant perfection; it is progressive restoration. There will be days when you feel the oppression again, but remember, they prove light still exists. The enemy may whisper, but you now know his voice. You have learned to detect his tone, to discern his lies, and to silence him with truth. You are not the victim anymore; you are the gatekeeper.

And when the enemy tries to remind you of your past, remind him of his future. When he points at your wounds, point at the Cross. When he accuses you of failure, declare, *"The Blood speaks better things."* Every breath you take is a declaration of defeat over hell. You are no longer prey; you are a living testimony that light is stronger than darkness.

Reflection Questions

1. Which of the steps in deliverance and maintenance feels most urgent for you right now?
2. What atmosphere fills your home and mind most often, peace or heaviness?
3. How can you make worship and Scripture meditation part of your daily rhythm?
4. Who can walk with you in accountability and prayer as you sustain your healing?

Key Takeaways

- Deliverance begins at awareness and continues through discipline.
- The atmosphere you create determines which spirit remains.
- Worship, prayer, and Scripture are not routines, they are weapons.
- Freedom is guarded by holiness and community.
- The mind can be renewed, and the soul can be refilled with light.

About the Author

Dennis Ofori is an anointed servant of the Lord Jesus Christ and a kingdom-minded author with over a decade of experience in prophetic, healing, and deliverance ministry. His writings carry prophetic depth and revelatory insight, awakening the Church to the realities of the spirit world and preparing believers for the second coming of Christ.

His books are written for Christians who seek serious, scripturally grounded answers to life's deepest questions, believers who have prayed, fasted, and obeyed yet still wrestle with delays, unanswered prayers, or spiritual battles.

Beyond ministry, Dennis is a seasoned cybersecurity and network engineering consultant with over two decades of professional experience. Internationally certified across multiple IT domains, he has trained and mentored professionals in penetration testing, IT Infrastructure Security, Cisco, VMware, Microsoft, and Linux technologies.

He bridges the spiritual and technological realms, empowering people to stand secure, both in the digital world and in the Kingdom of God.

Books by Dennis Ofori

The writings of Dennis Ofori call believers back to the ancient path of truth, holiness, and spiritual discernment. Each book carries a unique revelation, exposing deception and unveiling divine order in a confused world. To continue exploring these themes, visit the following titles available on Amazon:

1. Unmasking the Modern False Prophets: How to Discern and Guard Yourself Before It Is Too Late

Every generation faces deception, but ours hides behind charisma, miracles, and spiritual language. This book exposes how false prophets exploit signs, emotions, and spiritual hunger to lead believers into subtle manipulation. It reveals how deception disguises itself through charm, prophetic theatrics, and counterfeit fire. *Unmasking the Modern False Prophets* will train you to test the spirits, discern the source of supernatural manifestations, and guard your soul from manipulation disguised as prophecy. If you have been confused, wounded, or misled by so called prophets, this book will restore clarity, discernment, and peace.

2. Unmasking the Modern False Teachers: Guarding Your Faith in an Age of Twisted Doctrines and False Lights

False prophets deceive through experiences, but false teachers deceive through doctrine. This book exposes how corrupted teaching enters the pulpit through half-truths, motivational preaching, and grace without transformation. It reveals how Satan replaces holiness with entertainment and how doctrines that comfort the flesh quietly destroy spiritual foundations. This book will train you to distinguish between sound doctrine and seductive teaching. If you hunger for truth in a generation drowning in compromise, this book will strengthen your discernment and safeguard your walk with God.

3. Aligned In Purity: A Christian Guide to Freedom from Sexual Sin and the Journey of Transformation

Behind every immoral bond lies a spiritual covenant. This book reveals how sexual sin opens spiritual gates, binds destinies, and creates invisible altars that tie people to cycles of guilt, addiction, and spiritual oppression. It exposes the mechanics of soul ties, lust driven altars, and how unholy intimacy gives demonic forces legal access to the believer. *Aligned in Purity* is not a book of condemnation but a manual of deliverance. You will learn how to break soul ties, uproot lust driven covenants, restore purity, and reclaim your spiritual authority in Christ.

4. Delayed: Unveiling the Spiritual Intelligence Behind Delayed Answers to Strategic Prayers

Why does God delay? What happens when heaven is silent? This book uncovers the hidden operations of the spirit realm during seasons of delay and reveals how angels, obedience, faith, and warfare all play vital roles in answered prayer. *Delayed* will help you interpret divine silence, recognize demonic interference, and align yourself with heaven's timing. If you have prayed faithfully and still wondered why manifestation tarries, this book will turn your waiting into wisdom and victory.

5. The Dream Gate: Breaking the Power of Satanic Dreams and Awakening Divine Encounters

Dreams are spiritual gates. God uses them to warn, direct, and reveal destiny. Satan also invades the night to plant fear, confusion, lust, and manipulation. This book exposes how demonic forces operate in dreams and how believers can break cycles of night attacks, spiritual paralysis, and oppressive dreams. You will learn how to discern divine dreams, activate spiritual sensitivity during sleep, and protect your dream life with scriptural strategies. The night is not neutral. This book equips you to take dominion over it.

6. Destiny Actualization: The Spiritual Laws of Becoming Who God Designed

You were created for a divine purpose. This book reveals the spiritual laws that govern becoming everything God intended you to be. It exposes why many begin their spiritual journey with zeal but fail to reach divine fulfillment. Through biblical insight, you will learn how prayer, purity, obedience, and spiritual discipline align you with heaven's blueprint. If you sense a calling but feel hindered by fear, delay, or inner conflict, this book will break the barriers and help you walk in your full spiritual stature.

7. Spiritual Alignment: The Lost Principle of Divine Order — A Practical Guide to Unshakable Dominion

Heaven operates by order, not emotion. This book restores the forgotten principle of alignment, revealing how spiritual power flows through divine structure, submission, and obedience. Many believers have passion but lack order, which is why their strength collapses under pressure. You will learn how authority, answered prayer, spiritual stability, and dominion are all rooted in divine alignment. This book brings you back into the system of heaven where everything functions by order.

8. The Weight of Your Words: The Unseen Consequences of What You Say and Why It Matters

Every word is a seed. This book unveils how speech shapes spiritual realities, influences atmospheres, opens gates, and determines outcomes in a believer's life. Many pray for breakthroughs while their own words destroy the foundations of what they are asking God to build. The Weight of Your Words will teach you how careless speech invites defeat and how sanctified speech aligns heaven's resources with your destiny. Governing your world begins with governing your tongue.

9. Midnight Warfare: The Believer's Guide to Spiritual Dominance

Midnight is a spiritual gate. This book reveals why the hours between night and dawn are decisive in spiritual warfare. It teaches you how territorial spirits operate in darkness and how focused intercession at midnight can break generational patterns, overturn demonic agendas, and release angelic intervention. If you have experienced unexplained heaviness at night, sudden fear before dawn, or recurring oppression in the night season, this book will give you understanding and prayer strategies for victory.

10. Discernment and Betrayal: The Wisdom of Knowing a Person Beyond Appearance and Words

Deception often hides behind beauty, charm, and loyalty. This book reveals the spiritual gift of discernment and teaches you how to see beyond smiles, gestures, and impressive words. You will learn how to perceive intentions in the spirit, identify hidden traps, and avoid relational ambushes. In a world ruled by appearance and emotion, this book will protect you from betrayal and guide you into connections that align with God's will.

11. WHAT IF: Why Rejecting Jesus Christ Will Be the Greatest Tragedy in Your Existence

WHAT IF is not an argument. It is a mirror that confronts the soul with the weight of eternity. This book challenges intellectual skepticism, human pride, and the deception of unbelief by asking the questions no one wants to face: What if you are wrong about eternity? What if you are wrong about Jesus ? What if you are wrong about death? Etc. This book presents Christ not as religion but as reality. It will provoke deep reflection and compel the reader to reconsider the truth of salvation.

12. Before You Say Goodbye: Know the Hidden Truth Behind Suicide and the Spirit World

Many believe suicide ends suffering, but in the spirit realm it begins it. This book unveils the spiritual reality behind suicidal influence and exposes the demonic deception that convinces people to end their lives. Suicide is not escape. It is a doorway into deeper torment because the very spirit that pushed the person to die is waiting to continue the affliction beyond the body. This book brings clarity, compassion, and revelation. It helps you understand spiritual warfare around suicide and equips you to rescue yourself or others from this deadly illusion.

13. Beyond The Surface: His Spirit Will Tell You More Than His Appearance

People judge by appearance, but the spirit reveals truth. This book shows how relationships must be governed by spiritual discernment, not outward charm or personality. According to 2 Corinthians 5 verse 16, we are called to see beyond the surface. The Spirit of God reveals the true nature, future, and intentions of a person in ways human observation never can. This book trains you to pray until God unveils a person's character, motives, and destiny. Appearance is deceptive. The spirit never lies.

14. Humility: The Most Misunderstood Virtue in the Church

Humility has been mistaken for softness, quietness, or a gentle personality. This is false. The Bible teaches that humility is an inward condition of the heart, and only God can see it. Jesus said He was meek and lowly, yet meekness is external while humility is internal. Because man sees outwardly but God sees inwardly, no human being can truly determine who is humble. What we often call humility is actually meekness. This book exposes the confusion between meekness and humility and restores the true biblical meaning of humility as heaven defines it.

15. Anointing Without Foundation: The Crisis of Character in Anointed Men of God

Anointing opens doors, but only character keeps them open. This book reveals the growing crisis of ministers who carry spiritual power but lack internal stability. Hidden flaws, unhealed wounds, and unrefined character eventually crush the weight of their anointing. This book is a warning and a roadmap. It calls ministers to rebuild integrity, purity, accountability, and holiness beneath the power God has given them.

16. Your Child, The Target: The Parent's Warfare Manual

Children are the battlefield of the future. This book exposes how Satan uses media, culture, education, and entertainment to influence children away from God. It equips parents to stand as spiritual guardians, building walls of prayer, discernment, and authority around their homes. If you have ever felt the urgent need to pray for your child but didn't know where to start, this manual gives you the strategy, direction, and spiritual intelligence you need.

17. The Salvation Illusion: Escape the Deception of Easy Salvation in an Age of Mass Apostasy

Not every gospel leads to salvation. This book exposes the modern teaching that promises heaven without holiness, grace without surrender, and faith without obedience. It restores the fear of God, the truth of repentance, and the biblical standard of salvation that transforms the heart. If you desire truth beyond convenience, this book will pull you out of the comfort of false assurance and back into authentic Christianity.

18. Sour Grapes: Understanding and Breaking Free from Inherited Generational Cycles and Battles

Every generation of believers faces its own form of warfare. This book reveals how spiritual patterns, family covenants, generational weaknesses, and inherited battles continue through bloodlines even after salvation. Sour Grapes teaches you how to identify generational struggles, break inherited patterns, and establish a legacy of spiritual victory for your family.

19. The Manipulated Flock: Breaking Free from Coercive Control Within the Church

Spiritual authority was meant to liberate, not enslave. This book exposes how fear, guilt, intimidation, and religious control have replaced true shepherding in many churches. If you have felt trapped, controlled, or spiritually suffocated under the name of submission, this book will break the chains and restore your personal relationship with Christ.

20. Your Child, The Target: Protecting The Next Generation From Spiritual Warfare And Demonic Influence

this book expands the revelation from the first volume by unveiling the spiritual psychology behind how the enemy targets children. It exposes the demonic strategies hidden in media, peer culture, digital content, and educational ideologies designed to shape a child's identity away from God. You will learn how to counter these dark influences with prayer, wisdom, discernment, and intentional parenting. Every child is a seed of a future kingdom. This book shows you how to protect that seed.

21. Bloodline Access : Understanding How The Enemy Traces Families Through Ancient Covenants

Every covenant speaks through blood. This book reveals how bloodlines carry spiritual authority, how ancestral altars operate in families, and how certain battles continue from generation to generation until confronted by the power of Christ. *Bloodline Access* teaches you how to break demonic blood covenants, silence ancestral voices, and enforce the victory of the blood of Jesus over your life and lineage.

22. Holy Confusion: The Crisis of African Christian Weddings

Marriage is a covenant, not a performance. This book confronts how modern Christian weddings have become ceremonies of excess, competition, and pressure rather than holy covenants before God. Holy Confusion calls believers to return to purity, simplicity, and spiritual purpose. It corrects wrong foundations and restores the true meaning of the marriage altar.

www.ingramcontent.com/pod-product-compliance
Lightning Source LLC
LaVergne TN
LVHW090405210926
848480LV00002B/452